Nathalie Sarraute
COLLECTED PLAYS

By the same author

Novels
Portrait of a Man Unknown
Martereau
The Planetarium
The Golden Fruits
Between Life and Death
Do You Hear Them?
"Fools Say"

Short Prose and Criticism
Tropisms and *The Age of Suspicion*

Plays
Silence and *The Lie*

Nathalie Sarraute

COLLECTED PLAYS

It Is There, It's Beautiful, Izzum,
The Lie, Silence

Translated from the French by
Maria Jolas and Barbara Wright

JOHN CALDER
LONDON

Collected Plays first published in Great Britain, 1980, by
John Calder (Publishers) Ltd.,
18 Brewer Street,
London W1R 4AS

Originally published in France, 1978 as *Théâtre* by
Editions Gallimard,
5 rue Sebastien-Bottin,
75341 Paris

British Library Cataloguing in Publication Data

Sarraute, Nathalie
    Collected plays of Nathalie Sarraute.
    842'.9'14   PQ2637.A783A2

ISBN 0 7145 3713 6 hardback

Typeset in 9/10 pt Press Roman by Gilbert Composing Services, Leighton Buzzard
Printed by M. & A. Thomson Litho Ltd., East Kilbride
Bound by Hunter & Foulis Ltd., Edinburgh

CONTENTS

The plays in this collection have been broadcast (90 productions in all) in fifteen countries: France, Germany, Italy, Switzerland, The Netherlands, Sweden, Norway, Denmark, Finland, Czechoslovakia, Poland, Yugoslavia, Tunisia, Canada and Japan.

They have all been produced in the theatre.

It Is There

Translated by Barbara Wright

Elle est là (*It Is There*) was first performed on 15 January 1980 at the Théâtre d'Orsay by the Renaud-Barrault company and the Claude Régy Workshop, with the following cast:

MAN 1	Marc Eyraud
MAN 2	Roland Bertin
MAN 3	Jean-Claude Jay
WOMAN	Claude Degliane

M 1. I rather think that what we've been seeing recently is a recurrence . . . a progressive deterioration . . .

M 2. Yes . . . yes . . .

M 1. I was reading only the other day . . . He agreed with me . . . it's an irreversible trend . . .

M 2. Yes . . . that's very true . . .

M 1. What can you expect? All we can do is grin and bear it . . . No one, in any case . . . don't you think?

M 2. Yes yes, of course . . . I also think . . . But just a minute . . . let me . . . excuse me . . . I must . . . I'll be back in a moment . . . *(Exit. Re-enter.)* Too late: she isn't there.

M 1. Who isn't there?

M 2. It doesn't matter . . . only I'd have like . . . But she's already gone . . . Yes, the person who . . .

M 1. Was there something you had to say to her?

M 2. Yes, actually . . .

M 1. Couldn't you leave a message? . . . Call on her, telephone?

M 2. No, you know . . . it's, er . . . it's difficult . . . But it doesn't matter . . . Let's forget about it . . . You were saying, then?

M 1. Well, I was simply observing that in the present circumstances . . . given the way things are . . . But you don't look well . . . you're not your usual self . . . I'm disturbing you . . .

M 2. Not at all . . . On the contrary . . .

M 1. Say it straight out, I quite understand . . .

M 2. Oh no, there's no . . . No, I simply wanted . . . *(Silence.)* This is ridiculous . . . Listen . . .

M 1. Yes?

M 2. Just now, when we were arguing . . . well, you couldn't call it arguing, because we were in agreement . . . well, you and I were . . . whereas she . . . she was there while we were talking, she was listening . . .

M 1. Who was? Ah, that person? . . . Your assistant?

M 2. Yes . . . well, my colleague . . . but it really doesn't matter who she is . . . Did you see her expression? . . .

M 1. No, to tell you the truth I didn't . . .

M 2. You didn't notice? You didn't feel it? She didn't agree with us. But not in the slightest . . .

M 1. I must admit I wasn't really paying attention. But it's very likely.

M 2. Ha! 'Very likely!' Very. Very. Extremely. But I didn't react.

I let it . . . Why didn't I ask her? Yes, I should have . . .

M 1. Why? I don't understand . . . Does it matter *that* much—what she might think?

M 2. No . . . Yes . . . Well . . .

M 1. Hm . . . It's ȯdd . . . There's no doubt that she's a good person . . But to tell you the truth, she doesn't seem . . .

M 2. Oh, I know . . . She isn't a ball of fire . . . But what we were saying was really within the understanding of . . . you don't have to be a great intellectual . . . she's perfectly capable of making a judgment, isn't she, like everyone else . . . Well then, just knowing that it's there, in her . . . I don't know how to explain . . . It's there . . . Here . . . *(Brings two fingers up to his forehead.)* She has her little idea there . . . Why 'little', at that? I'm trying to reassure myself . . . She has her idea in her. An idea is there. Hidden. And ours, *our* idea, just now . . . got somehow caught up . . shut up in there, delivered up defenceless, strangled in silence, in secret . . . Nothing visible . . . I ought to have intervened . . . forced her to disclose it, to bring it out into the light of day . . . so that we could see her fine idea, which dared to attack . . . so that we could destroy it . . .

M 1. My poor friend, if you had to worry about . . . you have enough on your plate. I can see quite clearly what must be running through her head . . . and not only through hers, at that . . . It's an idea that's going around . . .

M 2. Going around? Yes, going around . . . going around . . . that's it . . . Something that's going around . . . it's proliferating . . . you find it everywhere . . . amongst every . . .

M 1. And you know: however hard you try, you'll never persuade them . . .

M 2. That's just it. That's just what I'm saying . . . It has an invincible force. That's how it is, with ideas. People they've taken root in acquire such certainty . . . such assurance . . . which is so exasperating . . . Didn't you notice? She had a sort of little smile . . . She thought we were to be pitied . . . I should have reacted immediately and provoked her, forced her . . . and I let it go . . . So now it's there . . . it is *there*, in her . . . a noxious animal . . . living, flourishing . . . no way of coming to grips with it, of . . .

M 1. Does this often happen to you? You must often have your work cut out . . .

M 2. No . . . In the ordinary way, thank God . . . I can't think of anything like it . . . It wasn't until today . . . she was there when we got on to the subject of . . . then immediately . . . something began to stir in her . . . and I let it . . . out of cowardice, lack of backbone . . .

M 1. Just as well. Can you see us preaching the gospel . . .

10

M 2. Yes, I know . . . But personally . . . *(Enter* W.*)* Ah, there you are,
I thought you'd gone . . . That's true, I don't know why, it isn't
late . . . Ah, that's good, the main thing is that you are here . . .
Stay a little longer . . . I must . . .

M 1. But I'm afraid it's time for *me* to go . . . I'm already . . .

M 2. Yes, I understand . . . Yes, see you soon, see you very soon . . .
we'll telephone . . . *(Exit* M 1.*)* Oh, you know, I must tell you . . .
I must speak to you . . .

W. Really? What about?

M 2. It's silly . . . it's very difficult . . . I don't know how . . . where
to start . . .

W. Never mind—go ahead. What have I done this time?

M 2. Oh, nothing. Nothing. That's just it—nothing. You did nothing.
You said nothing. You kept quiet . . .

W. Was I supposed to speak?

M 2. Yes, that would have been better . . .

W. To speak when? To speak about what? I don't understand.

M 2. Yes, yes . . . you'll see, you *will* understand . . . Just now, when
he was here, yes, that friend . . . when we were talking in front of
you, you remember, you'd come in . . .

W. Shouldn't I have?

M 2. But of course, of course, what are you . . . there was nothing
secret . . . it seemed to me . . . I felt . . . you didn't agree, did
you?

W. Well, perhaps not . . . but what of it?

M 2. Then you were wrong.

W. Really? you think so?

M 2. Do I *think* so? I'm quite sure of it. As wrong as can be.
What we were saying—it was ridiculous how obvious it was . . .

W. I don't agree.

M 2. You don't agree? But it's as plain as a pikestaff, can't you see
that? . . . and anything anyone has to say against it is just nebulous . . .
just nebulous nonsense . . .

W. Don't get so excited . . . What's the use? Let's forget about . . .

M 2. No, let us *not* forget about . . . certainly not, we mustn't . . .
excuse me, I really shouldn't get so excited . . . you'll see, I'm
going to keep calm . . . You'll see: what you think, it doesn't hold
water . . . it can't hold water. It's wrong . . . quite wrong . . . I
know where you got it from . . . you were force-fed . . . you
swallowed it whole . . . But all you need to do is examine it . . .
just think for a second . . .

W. Ah, because I don't think . . . Not ever? I'm force-fed, like a
goose. *You're* the only one . . . *You* 'think' . . . *You* 'know'. *Your*
'truths' are not 'swallowed whole', they compel recognition,
they are 'accepted'. And in any case, that's what I did . . .

I didn't give any sign . . . But that's still not enough . . . But where have we got to?

M 2. Yes, where have we got to? I'm crazy . . . That's what comes of . . of giving equal . . . of discussing . . . Oh no, don't go . . . I was wrong. There's no point in being aggressive. It's nothing to do with *us* . . . with *you* . . .

W. Nothing to do with us? Well well! . . . You're a fine one . . . 'Just think for a second'. 'You've been force-fed' . . . I'm an idiot, a half-wit . . . whom you're honouring by . . . and I'm supposed to put up with it . . . No but really—who do you take me for?

M 2. Oh . . . for someone very worth while, believe me . . . The proof of that is that I am trying to convince you . . . Your opinion, for me, as you can see . . .

W. Oh well, yes—that's true . . . But I can't help wondering why . . . What on earth does it matter to you what I think? You have *your* idea. I have mine. Don't we have a right . . .?

M 2. Of course, of course. A right. Every right. You have a right to have it. You can keep it. Circulate it . . . *(A slight pause.)* amongst people like you.

W. People like me? What do you mean by that? *(Turning to the audience.)* Did you hear him? People like you . . . The thing is that there are quite a few of us, aren't there? . . . What's so odd about us? . . .

M 2. Oh, nothing. Do let's forget about it. We're wandering . . . we're straying . . . Listen, my dear friend . . . No, that's not just an empty phrase. You *are* a friend—a real one. Then tell me . . . Answer me frankly . . . Just now, what we were saying . . . it came up against one of your convictions . . . I'd like to understand: it aroused a resistance . . . and yet it was self-evident . . .

W. No. Personally I think it didn't make sense.

M 2. It didn't make sense? What we were saying? Can't you see that we were simply pushing on an open door?

W. It wasn't open for me. Though no doubt I'm not open-minded.

M 2. But of course you are. Only you always have to . . . you can't . . . you always have to see everything in terms to yourself . . . that's all that matters.

W. Oh, look here, I've had enough. Tomorrow, then. That's right, isn't it?—tomorrow at ten? . . .

M 2. Yes, I know . . . But just a moment . . . Wait . . .

W. What am I supposed to wait for? No, but really, what do you want of me? What's the use? You'll never persuade me.

M 2. You see, you simply don't want to . . .

W. No, I don't want to. There's no point. I know what you're going to say, and it gets on my nerves.

M 2. It gets on your nerves, does it? Well then, I'm going to get on

12

your nerves. You're going to be forced to listen to it. I'll get it into your head whether you like it or not. *(He shouts some unintelligible words. She covers her ears. He removes her hands.)* It—will—get—in . . . Yes, even here, in this . . . this . . . *(He taps her forehead)* . . . It isn't possible for it not to penetrate, not to demolish what is in there, that stupid nonsense.

W.   But look here . . . what's got into you? what's the matter with you? You must have lost your head. *(Exit.)*

M 2 *(alone).*   Stuck-up creature. Moron. You'd have to have a real urge to commit yourself . . . to compromise yourself . . . Her idea . . . no, really, I ask you . . . Right—let her keep it. It won't change the face of the world . . . It won't change . . . *(Addressing the audience.)* Really . . . you think so? Is that possible? you think it *can* change the face of the world, just that . . . that little idea tucked away in her . . . hidden . . . Oh, if only you felt like coming up here, with me . . . to tell me . . . to explain how . . . why . . . I really don't know . . . But I feel it's essential that what is there, in her, must be destroyed, extracted, crushed . . . No? You don't agree? Then I was wrong. You *don't* agree that it can change the face of the world . . . that it can endanger . . . What have I been imagining? . . . This is so absurd . . . *(Silence. To the audience.)* I know very well what you'd say to me if you did feel like speaking, I know what would be on the tip of your tongues . . . It's what everyone says to himself in cases like mine . . . when it gets hold of you, when it takes possession of you . . . that sort of obsession . . . there's only one way to get rid of it: think of something else. They say that one nail drives out another, don't they. And there's no shortage of nails, here. There's even a surfeit of them: nice, big fat nails . . . *(A silence.)*

(Jovially.) Hm—I have one, too. A magnificent one. *(Concentrates.)* There. I'll drive it in . . . There. I think that's it . . . *(Silence, then he writhes and groans.)* . . . No, it's no use . . . it's there, stuck fast in me, her idea . . . it's pushing, it's pressing . . . it hurts. But isn't there *anyone* here . . . is there *no one* who would agree to . . . Oh!

(Enter a character—M 3—dressed up to look like the archetypal petit bourgeois.) Oh, you . . . Have you come to my assistance? Well, really . . . Just the very sight of you makes me feel better . . . But maybe I'm rejoicing too soon . . . Excuse me, but may I ask you . . . You aren't the policemen on duty, are you? Or one of the other house officials? An attendant? The doctor? No, you came here to enjoy yourself, to be entertained, 'to have a nice evening'. Yes, I'm sorry . . . it's true that so far as entertainment goes . . . I do realise that we could do better . . . Still, what can you expect? . . . But perhaps even so you are a doctor by profession . . . a psychiatrist, perhaps . . . Because, you know, however much I may

13

be suffering, I wouldn't want them to try to 'cure' me for anything in the world. Oh no, no thank you, not for this one, expecially not that sort of cure, thank you very much. Because when someone has . . . symptoms . . . like these . . . they feel it their bounden duty to bring him back to normal. And what they consider 'normal' . . . No, I much prefer . . . But you aren't one? Well . . . you reassure me. *(Observes him in silence.)*

But . . . just one more question. As you see, I'm suspicious. Once bitten, you know. It's that you seem so . . . so respectable . . . so well-balanced, that anyone looking at you might think . . . well, no one would think that you . . .too . . . that you could be someone . . . like me . . . But how foolish I am . . . If you were what you seemed to be at first sight, you would certainly have kept quiet, safe and sound down there, in the dark . . . not so mad . . . well, not mad enough to come up here and lay yourself open to . . . you'd be with the rest of them . . . the ones who refuse, who won't commit themselves . . . you might even be one of the ones who walk out, who have had more than enough . . . But you, you have the courage . . . You . . . Appearances are deceptive. It isn't the cowl that makes the monk. How true . . . Oh, come over here, come closer . . . tell me . . . not out loud, if it makes you feel self-conscious . . . no, just in a whisper, here in my ear . . . that's all I ask. (M 3 *whispers in his ear.)* Ah, you understand me . . . It happens to you too, an idea tucked away in almost anyone . . . really? . . . even in a child, sometimes? . . . yes, it does, doesn't it? it can get you into such a state . . . But am I dreaming? It can't be true. It can't be happening to me . . . because, you know, no one ever . . . and now you! Oh . . . you're like me. You're the same. And completely normal, aren't you? perfectly correct. Nothing of the eccentric about you. Impeccably turned out. Respectability itself . . . Well then, it's . . . *(Silence.)* Well yes *(to the audience)* you see, miracles do sometimes occur. Just when you least expect them. It would be enough to make you believe . . . that's to say . . . personally, it can't be helped, I'm not a believer . . . *(becomes silent.)*

Well then, you see, now there are two of us. Two—that's already a force. Two. Someone else like me. That changes everything. As somebody or other said in some play or other . . . I think it was a clown: 'That changes absolutely everything'. I am no longer alone. What a relief. Now we can examine the situation calmly and with lucidity. That stuck-up creature . . . No, I mustn't say that, that's cheating . . . That 'person'. That 'human being' . . . it's odd to say that, but it's necessary. It must be said, and repeated; a human being, it doesn't matter who, carries within himself—or herself— an idea which destroys . . . yes, which by its very existence . . . hm? we do agree . . . oh my goodness, what luck . . . an idea which by its very existence threatens . . . yes, let us dare to pronounce the word: the truth . . . so it's intolerable, so we must extract it, extricate it, we must destroy it . . . we cannot allow it to . . . it's a dangerous germ . . . we must disinfect . . . cleanse . . .

M 3 *nods his agreement, then abruptly moves away, looks up into the air and seems to catch something like a fly in his hand. It is a little paper ball.*

M 2. What is it? Show me. What did they throw us?

M 3 *unfolds it, looks at it and passes it to* M 2.

M 2 *(reads, is perplexed, and scratches his head.)* In—to—le—rance. Intolerance. Hm, they're a fine lot, down there. Just one word tossed up like that . . . it's staggering. What we are doing here is quite simply called intolerance. Which is absolutely forbidden by our laws. Just look . . . running through their heads, behind their staring eyes . . . you can see . . . words like film subtitles . . . can you read them?'Freedom of thought', 'Respect for other people's opinions', 'We live in a democracy'. What were we going to do, eh, you and I? When nobody could be more democratic! The moment they start attacking our liberties, you and I, eh? . . . we see red. *(Laughs.)* You see where such ready-made phrases can get you— somewhere you never meant to go . . . No, let's rather say that they make your hair stand on end . ... In—to—le—rance. Yes, there's nothing to be done, we must give up.

He stands there with bowed head, distressed.

M 3 *(leaning over towards* M 2). It's awkward . . . We're up against it, I think. We have no right to attack that poison . . .

M 2. Yes—to see it at work, and not do anything. Tolerance. We're bogged down in it . . . bound hand and foot . . . What a word, eh? A real strait-jacket . . .

Distressed silence.

But look here . . . what's the matter with us? We're losing our heads. I won't allow myself to be hamstrung like this. Tolerance? But I repeat: no one is more tolerant than you and I. Freedom of thought? Excellent. Respect for others? Fine. *(To the audience.)* But free discussion - what do you make of that? Don't you allow it? Ah, you see, of course they allow it. But then? . . . For our part, you know, that's all we ask: free discussion. Liberty. Equality. Fraternity. Fraternally, in all equality, without paying the slightest attention to the slightest difference, in the most total liberty, we want to enter into a discussion, a battle of ideas . . . but perfectly prepared to admit . . . no? . . .

M 3. Oh, I'd even go so far as to say that I'd like nothing better than to be proved wrong.

M 2. Yes, it's odd, but so would I; it would be a relief. The thing is— as I was telling you—no one could be less bigoted than we, less fanatic . . . Did you notice? It was she who refused to discuss . . . I tried . . . and she snubbed me, did you notice how she did it?

M 3. But you *were* actually rather abrupt with her . . . I think it would have been better to approach her a little more tactfully . . .

M 2. Yes, more tactfully. That's right. Very tactfully. And especially, not antagonize her. Not arouse her suspicions.

M 3. Ask her to come in . . . You can find a way.

M 2. Oh, nothing could be simpler. Any pretext will do. *(Goes and opens the door and puts his head through it. W enters and comes up.)* May I introduce . . . this is a friend.

W. Do you need me?

M 2. Oh yes. Yes . . . I was just telling this friend how I can't possibly do without you. The moment you leave me I feel lost . . .

W. Is that true?

M 3. It's perfectly true: he was telling me how much it counts . . . how much he relies on you . . . on your opinion . . .

W *(suspiciously)*. On my opinion?

M 2 & M 3 *(in chorus)*. No no, not exactly that . . .

M 2 *(resolutely)*. But on the other hand— yes: we must face facts. It's incredible to what an extent everything you think . . .

M 3. Oh yes, if you only knew to what an extent . . . He attaches such importance . . .

W. That's odd. Because personally, you know, I thought . . .

M 2 & M 3 *(avidly)*. Yes? You thought? . . .

W. I thought, quite simply, that he couldn't bear anyone, even me, venturing to . . .

M 2. Oh, what a mistake . . . On the contrary, that's all I ask— that you should venture to . . .

W. Are you sure? Could you bear it if I had my own little angle on . . .

M 2. Her own little angle . . . how sweet. Her own little angle . . . such modesty . . . Well, that little angle . . . if you wanted . . .

M 3. Personally, I don't accept that word.

M 2. He's right. Why not be frank and say: opinion?

W. Very well. Fine. But we aren't going to start all over again, are we? Not now. In any case, I've too much to do . . . there are some urgent matters . . .

M 2 & M 3 *(get up and block her way. Very gently, mealy-mouthed)*. Yes, yes, it *must* be now. We can't wait any longer. But don't be afraid. We don't wish you any harm. On the contrary. Come over here. We're so fond of you. Come over to us. Here, there . . .

M 3. No?—not between us? You don't want to? Well then, sit here, by me. (W *looks at* M 3.) Don't tell me I frighten you.

W.   Frighten me? No. Oh no . . . Only . . .

M 2.   Only what? If it's your work, it can wait . . . I'll answer for that . . .

M 3.   Come on, I'm sure you won't refuse to waste a little time with us . . . And you'll see, you'll even come to enjoy it. It will be we who have to cut you short, remind you that there are urgent tasks . . .

M 2 *(all smiles).*   Yes indeed.

M 3.   Do it for his sake. He's so fond of you, you know . . . and has been for such a long time . . . His affection for you is so . . .

M 2.   It's true. How long have we been working together now?

W *(coquettishly).*   Oh, I'd rather not think. It doesn't make us any younger . . .

M 2.   So you see: to start with, you're going to make your *amende honorable.* You're going to recite your *mea culpa.*

W.   Oh, really! . . . But why? . . .

M 2.   Because of what you just said: yes, that I didn't allow you to have your own opinion . . .

W.   Which is true.

M 2 & M 3.   But when? But tell us: when?

W *(says nothing).*

M 2 & M 3.   Come on, just a little effort . . . Wasn't there something only recently? . . .

W.   No. For goodness' sake . . .

M 2.   You see, it really is a question of the mote and the beam. *You*'re the one who doesn't want, freely, calmly, to . . . *You*'re the one who is refusing.

W.   Oh no . . . Or I shall go.

M 2.   That's a bit much . . . When I remember our discussions . . .

W.   Which ones?

M 2.   Well, let's say . . . the ones on education. Do you remember?

W *(confidently).*   Oh yes.

M 2.   I was in favour of authority. *(To* M 3.) And you know, she finally convinced me. She produced evidence. *(To* W.) You see, that time it was I who was . . .

W.   Who was what?

M 3.   Be careful. *(To* W.) Then he really did give in? Well, you know, you are to be congratulated. Because it's a fact that no one could be more obstinate . . . When he gets an idea into his head . . .

W.   Oh, then, yes . . . Well now, I really must . . .

M 2.   No, there's nothing you *must* . . . Nothing except answer me. And just tell me why . . . Yes, why so much injustice? Such a lack of reciprocity?

W.   I don't understand . . .

M 2.   Of course you do, you understand perfectly, a clever little thing like you . . . On that question about education, when I gave way, after I'd listened to your arguments, it was at least as serious . . .

W.   As serious as what?

M 2.   As serious as it was just now, when you rejected me . . . when I was begging you . . .

W.   Oh-oh—here we go again. I should have expected it. I should have been on my guard. That's how he always starts . . . in a very roundabout way, very cautiously, so as to get what he wants . . . so as to lead you by the nose . . .

M 2.   What nose? What are you talking about? I simply want reciprocity. Perfect equality. All I'm asking you to do is answer me . . .

M 3 *(very gently).*   Yes . . . answer him . . .

M 2 *(gently).*   Tell us why you refuse to accept . . . when it's so obvious true? What is it you've got into your head?

M 3.   Have the courage of your convictions.

W.   The courage? There's no need for courage. I'm not the only one. There are some extremely well-informed people. Very well-known. It would make them laugh if they knew we were arguing about . . .

M 2.   Laugh! It would make them laugh? Well then, make me laugh with them, that's all I ask . . . let's laugh together . . .

W.   Did you hear the way you said that? Just listening to you . . . brr! .

M 2.   Yes, brr, brr, brr . . . that's all you can find to answer me . . . You don't dare come out with that nonsense, those dishonest . . . And to think that I asked her to expose them . . . You certainly have to have a thick skin. A strong stomach.

W.   Ah, at last . . . now it's quite clear . . . this time I think you really will allow me . . .

Exit W. Silence.

M 2.   There we are, then. And I'm supposed to live at close quarters with *that* . . . with *that* tucked away in here, ensconced there . . . knowing that it's in there, permanently there, in a corner . . . like the idea of death, ever-present, somewhere in the background, whatever you do . . .

M 3.   Well, yes . . . But believe me, you ought to count your blessings. What if she were your wife? . . . Just think of that, the torture . . .

M 2.   Oh, I don't know . . . If she were my wife, it would be more than likely that on that level . . . When it comes to ideas, you know, it's like the conjugal domicile: up till now, what usually happens is that the wife follows . . .

M 3.   That's true . . . and when they do, it's often with such intransigeance, such fervour . . . they put their whole hearts into it . . .

M 2.   And anyway, you know, it seems that in some countries . . . well, in America, for instance . . . behaviour like hers would be grounds for divorce. Yes, really: for mental cruelty. It's provided for by the law.

M 3. To be quite honest . . . I don't know . . . but I think people might say that when it comes to cruelty . . . it's you, rather . . . she, poor thing—all she's doing is avoiding the issue; all she wants is to keep quiet . . .

M 2. That's true.

M 3. And then, as you well know, even in the case of a separation. it could still operate from a distance.

M 2. Oh! so it could! From a distance. It's enough to know that it's there, that it's still there in her, huddling in her head . . . and the moment one of *our* beautiful little ideas, a good, fresh, wholesome idea, began to take shape, to spread its wings . . . then we would immediately feel, coming from over there . . .

M 3. Yes, and even from a long way off, something stretching out its . . . Hm? Isn't that it?

M 2. Our idea would be trapped, bedraggled, hemmed in, there—slobbered over, flattened, crushed . . . As if, there . . . as if a boa-constrictor . . .

M 3. Personally, I see it more like a little machine, a sort of pulverizing mechanism, that automatically . . .

M 2. That's it: automatically. A blind force. You can foretell, you can foresee . . .

M 3. There's a mechanism, in that brain, and it is au-to-ma-ti-cally going to seize, pulverize, reduce to dust, to a pulp . . .

M 2. . . . something that breathes . . . something that wants to live . . . And there's nothing we can do to stop it.

M 3. We simply can't move . . .

Silence.

M 2. And yet, it's certainly a case of breaking that law—a case of refusing assistance to a thought in danger . . . isn't it? And that's serious . . .

Silence.

M 3. Very serious. Unacceptable. Intolerable.

M 2. Unfortunately, though, if we want to come to its aid— to come to the aid of our thought in danger—I see no other way than . . .

M 3. I know. That's what I was thinking too . . . It's the only possible way of permanently preventing that dormant boa entrenched in her head . . . or, if you prefer, that mechanism . . .

M 2. That's right: No more irresistible boa-attacks.

M 3. No more automatic movements.

M 2 & M 3. Everything will be inert. Broken for ever. Destroyed.

M 2. Yes, but how? Broken how? How—destroyed for ever?

M 3. Obviously, if we could have at our disposal . . . you know . . .

19

the famous push-button that kills the mandarin . . .

M 2 *(irritably)*. Of course—but we haven't got it.

M 3. Then we must make up our minds . . . What can you . . . nothing is for nothing . . .

M 2. And this time, in the greatest solitude. Really alone, you and me. Not even anyone to throw us a little paper ball like they did just now . . . they're all too far away from us . . . And very far from that.

M 3 *(to the audience)*. Is that true? Are you so far away? Such a very long way off? Really? But how can that be? After everything that has happened? After everything that's been done . . . by people no one would ever even have thought . . . people like you and me . . . and by such a host of people . . . and on such an enormous scale . . . all the wars of religion . . . the inquisition, the stake, the gallows, the garotte, execution squads, charnel-houses and concentration camps? Really? Can't you understand?

Silence.

M 2. No: there's nothing to be done. *They* aren't like that. Very exceptional, you can see. Very pure. Non of them has ever . . . not even in their nightmares . . . No one here, that's right, isn't it?

So that's that. Just us alone. When I told you that there was something miraculous about your apparition . . . Just the two of us: just you and me . . . We must resign ourselves to that.

M 3. Then . . . What have you in mind? What do we do next?

M 2. Oh, nothing particularly original, as you may well imagine . . .

M 3. Yes, but even so: what?

M 2. Well then—turn on the gas in the heater in her office . . . or set fire to . . . Fake a burglary . . . Creep up behind her with a bit of rope or a scarf . . . Or a dagger, a hatchet . . . I don't know.

M 3. Yes indeed—in so far as imagination . . .

M 2. What do you expect?—one does what one can.

M 3. Well, those are just details. What matters . . .

M 2. Yes—is the result. *That*'s all that matters. Personally, just the very thought of it makes me start laughing like an idiot. Can you see the picture? A lovely little idea, born in us, fresh-blown . . . sparkling with truth, a dragon-fly, a beautiful butterfly . . . even in the presence of that person it could emerge with perfect impunity, flutter, settle wherever it wished . . . Yes, settle over there on that head . . .

M 3. That dead head .

M 2. Flutter in front of those eyes.

M 3. Yes, those closed eyes . . . closed for ever.

M 2. Penetrate those deaf ears. Tickle that inert little brain.

M 3. Not the slightest reaction. Never more.

M 2.   And then—total disappearance. Nothing left. Barely a memory.

Silence.

Unfortunately, in our case . . . with our limited means . . . poor artisans
that we . . .

M 3.   Artisans! . . . it would be perfectly all right if . . . I was saying to
myself only a moment ago: what a terrible, botched-up job . . .

M 2.   Naturally . . . with absolutely no help . . . No state aid. And to
think that there are so many countries where the state takes care
of these things successfully, too. But here, well, it's every man for
himself. At his own risk.

M 3.   And what a risk . . .

M 2.   I can just see us . . . trying to explain to the examining
magistrate . . .

M 3.   And our defence at the Assize Court . . . pleading 'Assistance
to a thought in danger' . . .

M 2.   Which the law does *not* provide for . . .

Silence

Ah, all this is a dream . . . Our little moment of wishful thinking . . .

Silence.

M 3.   You know, what comforts me . . . is that in the end, all that
work . . . that enormous risk . . .

M 2.   I know: it wouldn't do us much good: just give us a little
temporary relief. The ignoble thing . . . That filthy little . . . that
boa . . . we'd find it coiled up somewhere else . . . in another
head . . . and there's no shortage of heads . . .

M 3.   How true. There are as good fish in the sea . . .

Silence.

M 2.   It isn't the head that needs to be destroyed, it's the idea . . .
Not the carrier . . . but the idea he carries . . . the idea alone . . .

M 3.   Yes, to be purged . . . Cleansed. To clear the decks . . .

M 2.   And afterwards, in that same place, in that same head, we
could instil . . . spreading outwards . . . increasing and multiplying . . .

M 3.   Illuminating everything around . . .

M 2 & M 3 *(in the same breath).*   . . . the truth . . .

Silence.

M 3.   You know, that's what they call . . . *they*, over there, they have
words for everything, ready-made words . . . if they wanted to
have another try at calming us down . . . if they wanted to put
things back in their place, to put *us* in our place . . . they could tell
us that what we are after is quite simply an 'abjuration', followed
by a 'conversion'. We aren't the first . . .

M 2.   Yes, that's true, when you think of . . . But that's not going
to stop me . . . I haven't the slightest desire to be an innovator . . .
but what's really holding me back is that we have already, just now,
er, tried . . .

M 3.   Just now, we didn't know how to go about it. You got excited.
This time you must try to control yourself. Remember: no aggression
towards the carrier . . . nothing aimed at her personally. What we have
to do is destroy her idea. Destroy it utterly . . . With another idea . .
our idea . . . attacking hers . . .

M 2.   A war of ideas . . . and ours, by its sheer strength . . . must be
able to . . .

M 3.   Yes: triumph . . . no matter where. Even there. Bring her back.

M 2.   Who?

M 3.   The carrier, of course. Ideas, as you well know, need carriers . . .

M 2.   Of course. Excuse me, I don't know what I was thinking of . . .
But the carrier . . . I'm afraid that this time . . . The moment she
realizes that it has nothing to do with work . . . well, not with what
is normally called 'work' . . . Let's go to her, rather. We'll go in as
if nothing had happened . . .

M 3.   Yes, just sort of casually . . . Chance it and trust to God . . .

Exeunt, then re-enter.

M 3.   Well, are you satisfied? At least we managed to . . .

M 2.   Yes . . .

M 3.   You look disappointed . . . And yet we did a good job. Especially
me . . . Because you . . . There were moments, at the start, when I
was afraid you were going to back down . . .

M 2.   I'm sorry . . . just the very sight of her . . . sometimes, just the way
she looks, or smiles . . . I can't resist it . . . there's something so good
so . . .

M 3.   Yes, we know: she's a good woman . . . be we had decided that
'she' had nothing to do with it. It was the *idea* that was . . .

M 2.   Well then, there's cause for rejoicing: she *has* abjured her idea,
she *has* dismissed it . . . and in its place she has installed . . .

M 3.   Yes: the facts. Certainty. She accepted it . . . And she wasn't
only paying lip-service . . .

M 2.   No . . . not lip-service . . . But . . .

M 3.   What service, then?

M 2.   Well . . . when we went in, did you notice? . . .

M 3.   I noticed the back of her neck in the lamplight . . . It reminded
me of our plans . . .

M 2.   Not me: I found it touching. Something so innocent . . . so
defenceless . . .

M 3.   You put your hand on her shoulder, gently . . . affectionately . .

M 2.   And then, did you notice?

22

M 3. I noticed how she started—there was nothing extraordinary about that, she wasn't expecting it—she turned round, she put her hand to her heart, she said: 'Oh, you frightened me . . . '

M 2. And is that all? Didn't you notice anything else?

M 3. No, nothing.

M 2. Well—I know her. She understood everything at that moment. Yes, she saw everything in a flash . . . what we wanted . . . what she might expect . . . and then . . .

M 3. And then what?

M 2. It's easy to guess: immediately, on the spot, she made her decision. She decided to surrender.

M 3. You think so?

M 2. I'm sure of it.

M 3. It doesn't seem very plausible to me. She would have given in more quickly.

M 2. Did it seem long to you? She had to drag it out a bit, you must see that . . . that was mere child's play . . . she had to show us that, with the greatest reluctance, and convinced by the irresistible force of our arguments . . . that was the only way she could get rid of us, stop us returning to the charge . . .

M 3. No, wait a moment . . . Let's just think . . . When you started your overtures . . . beginning in a roundabout way, creeping up stealthily . . . there I must say I admired you . . . She let you get . . .

M 2. Yes, and then, when I had come out into the open . . . and you tell me that I didn't do a thing, that it was much more you . . . However . . . that's not the point . . . So, when I engaged the action, she . . .

M 3. She didn't seem to be giving ground.

M 2. No. As I have already said, she didn't want to give in immediately. She took her precautions, first . . . she picked up her idea, quickly put it aside, hid it in a corner . . . a cupboard where she locked up her little darling, out of reach of our attacks . . . and then she let us advance, putting up a bit of a sham defence . . .

M 3. At one moment, though, she stood up . . . I was already preparing to block her way . . .

M 2. There was no need. She sat down again.

M 3. Yes, that's true.

M 2. It was only a reflex action.

M 3. Yes, a gesture of rebellion, perhaps . . . She must have thought . we were overdoing it. Don't be offended, but it was at the moment when it looked as if . . . after all, she is rather dependent on you . . .

M 2. You're dreaming, she couldn't have thought that . . . I, use such methods . . . she knows me too well . . .

M 3. I know: I'm only saying that she might have imagined . . .

M 2. Nothing at all. There was a moment when she . . . what can you expect, it's only human . . . she couldn't help it . . . she thought she would escape and take her beloved idea with her. The little darling must have been getting impatient, it must have started knocking on the door, wanting to be let out of its hiding place . . . But she made it keep quiet, she sat down again meekly, ready to put up with everything to the bitter end. The moment her idea was safely tucked away, where no one could get at it . . .

M 3.   You're probably right. She seemed to be amused when she was watching you parade your arguments. The funniest thing was when you asked me to give you some facts . . . Quickly . . .

M 2.   Ah, and what facts, eh? a formidable battery . . .

M 3.   I was watching you stepping up the pressure. Increasing it . . . And you know, at that moment I really felt she was beginning to weaken. I thought she was becoming really open, to let the truth enter . . . To let it penetrate her all over . . .

M 2.   All over? But not in that well-protected little corner cupboard where her little idea was huddling . . . Believe me, anyone might say that we were lashing the waves. But there weren't even any waves. We were mustering all our strength to beat the void . . . Her own idea *is there*, intact. I'm sure that by now it has already crept out of its hiding place . . . and is attacking the lovely, great big truths that we have accumulated and left behind us . . . it's snaring them with bird-lime, it's coiling itself around them, it's hugging them . . . *(Groans.)* Oh, look . . . there . . .

M 3.   What is it?

M 2.   It's the carrier . . . *(Enter W. She starts doing things at a table, tidying papers, etc.)*

M 2 *(very softly).*   She still has it in her, you know.

M 3 *(very softly).*   You're right. It's still there in her, her idea . . . intact . . . not changed by a single iota . . . You can see that right away . . . just by that look . . .

M 2.   Yes, obstinate, inscrutable, narrow-minded, self-confident, oh . . . *(Groans.)*

M 3.   And secretive. It's exactly what you might call 'standing on your dignity'.

M 2 *(groans, and stands up).*   Oh, hold me back . . .

M 3.   Come come, get a grip on yourself, keep calm . . .

M 2 *sits down again. Exit W. Silence.*

M 2.   You know, I can't imagine what's happening to me . . . it's odd . . . *(Looking surprised.)* I accept. Yes. *(Furiously.)* I accept. *(Despondent* I accept. *(More calmly.)* I accept. *(Resolutely.)* I accept. Let her keep her idea in her. Let her incubate it. Let her nurse it. Let her fatten it . . . it's all the same to me . . .

M 3.   It's not possible! . . . Don't tell me you've become indifferent . . . apathetic . . . one of those people for whom ideas . . .

M 2.   Oh come! how can you think that . . . No, not in the least.

M 3. In that case, so as not to suffer any more, maybe you've found a nail that has driven out . . . ? A nice, big fat nail?

M 2. Oh no, no nails. Nothing has been able to drive out . . . *my* idea is still there. As the saying goes: I am 'possessed' by it . . . And yet I do accept that the other one, hers, over there, should live . . .

M 3. Ah, then you're resigned. A man can do no more than he can, eh?

M 2. No, not at all, you're mistaken.

M 3. What can't be cured must be endured?

M 2. No no, it's not that . . .

M 3. You're putting a good face on it?

M 2. No, you're on the wrong tack altogether. You'd better give up.

M 3. All right: I give up.

M 2. Well then, let me tell you that I'm pleased. Perfectly satisfied. That's all I ask: that she should have hers, and I should have mine. Every man for himself, and God for us all. No more extracting anything from anyone. No more incursions.

M 3. But look here: that's what they call 'tolerance'. Ah, I know some people down there *(pointing to the audience)* who'll be pleased. No need to throw us any more little paper balls to appeal to our better nature. *You're* the one who's setting the example now . . .

M 2. What? That again—tolerance? Always these words that hem you in, that deform . . . Just because I said that *her* idea may as well live, and grow fat, people immediately think that everything is back to normal. That it's tolerance . . . Well no, it isn't that at all. All I'm thinking of is *my* idea, and that alone . . . I don't want it to be debased any more . . . no more repugnant contacts, hand to hand fighting . . . I want us to be left alone, me and it. All alone.

Silence.

I'm sorry, I didn't mean to offend you, it's awkward to have to say that, to you . . . you've been so kind, so patient . . . and I've trespassed so much . . . But now, you see, I don't need any more help . . . I don't need anyone's support. That's the only thing we need, now: to be alone, all alone, my idea and I. And it might even . . . it's funny . . . you see how people change . . . it might even help us if you were against us . . . Yes, that's the way it is. If everyone were against us. You. The friend who was here earlier . . . and in any case, how can I know whether, when he was agreeing, he wasn't merely being polite . . . or lazy . . . and you yourself, maybe . . . just being kind . . . you never know . . . But it's all over. No more need to sound out their guts and hearts. Yes, everyone against . . . And they too, there . . . Just to imagine it . . . it's strange . . . it does me good . . . But I'm not imagining it . . . I feel that they have granted me my wish . . . Which, in any case, is one

25

of the ones that are usually most likely to be fulfilled. Look at them. See where they are, where they are sitting, at such a distance at a distance that can't be crossed by sympathy, or any sort of connivance. Those fixed, staring looks . . .

Silence.

It's funny, I believe I'm only now beginning to understand for the first time . . . A little thing, a tiny, unimportant little thing, sometimes leads you to the last place you would ever have thought you'd get . . . to the very depths of solitude . . . into cellars, casemates, cells, tortures, when the guns are levelled, when the barrel of the revolver is pressed against the back of your neck, when the rope is coiled, when the axe is about to fall . . . at the so-called supreme moment . . . it draws itself up with such violence . . . it bursts out of its shattered shell, it spreads, it, the truth . . . pure truth . . . it alone . . . by its mere existence it orders . . . everything around it, gently, nothing resists it . . . everything around it finds its own order . . . it illuminates *(the lights start to dim)* . . . such clarity . . . such order . . . Ah, it's here . . . this is the moment . . . this is the end . . . But only for me, but I am nothing, *I* don't exist . . . and it, with such strength . . released from that broken shell, it rises up, it frees itself, it spreads . . . it illuminates . . . *(the lights dim)* . . . no one can . . . that's how it is . . . no one can do anything to prevent it . . . we all know it, *(the lights dim)* don't we, we all say it: Truth always prevails . . . we need never fear for it . . . ah, it's well able to look after itself . . . *(the lights go out)* by its existence alone . . . by its presence alone . . . alone . . . all alone . . . so alone . . .

It's Beautiful

Translated by Maria Jolas

C'est beau (It's Beautiful) was first performed in October 1975 at the Théâtre d'Orsay with the following cast:

HE	Jean-Luc Bideau
SHE	Emmanuelle Riva
THEIR SON	Daniel Berlioux

Voices of MRS. DENNISON, MR DENNISON and others.

Directed by Claude Régy

HE. It's beautiful, don't you think so?

SHE *(hesitant)*. Ye-es . . .

HE. You don't think it's beautiful?

SHE *(as though reluctantly)*. Yes . . . Yes . . .

HE. What's the matter with you?

SHE. Oh, nothing. What do you expect? You asked me the question . . . and I answered yes . . .

HE. But the way you said it . . . mere lip service . . . As if it were such a concession. *(Worried.)* You don't like it?

SHE. Of course I like it, I told you so . . . But just now . . . you really don't want to understand . . .

HE. The fact is, no, I don't understand . . .

THEIR SON. Oh, listen, why pretend? You know that's all you'll ever get . . . lip service . . . a dull voice . . . that's all . . . absolutely all, and you know it. Since I'm here . . . And I don't even have to appear, there's no need even to say 'hoo-ooh', there he is . . . It's enough for me to be on the other side of the wall . . . shut up in my room . . . Even on the other side of a cement wall, my very presence would keep her from saying 'it's beautiful' the way you'd like her to say it . . .

HE. But what's got into you? What's he talking about? Is he crazy?

THEIR SON. Crazy? Me? Still the same old defensive reflexes, the same evasions, the same disguises . . . To deceive whom? Let's start over again . . . Just to see . . . I'll go to my room . . . And you will repeat it, you will say the way you did before: 'It's beautiful', isn't it? Don't you think so?

HE. Are you making fun of me! . . . How dare you? You little good-for-nothing . . .

THEIR SON. There we have it, it's contagious, you too have caught it. You felt it . . . You're backing down. You don't dare. The word sticks in your throat . . . It's beautiful. Beautiful. Beautiful. How beautiful it is! . . . Impossible, isn't it? You can't do it . . .

SHE. That's true, he's right. You see yourself . . . you don't dare . . .

HE. So you too are going crazy. I don't dare! I can't say 'It's beautiful'. in front of him. Just because he's present, that little ass. We'll see. Beautiful. Beautiful. Extremely beautiful! Excrutiatingly beautiful. Beautiful!

SHE. Oh, stop, please be quiet.

THEIR SON. Just to hear him is more than she can bear. That makes her panic, doesn't it? She would like to stop her ears . . . hide . . .

HE *(waking-up)*. What's happening anyway? Where are we? What are you talking about? To begin with, who is 'she'? Who are you talking about? Go on, get out, get going, you're disturbing us. Have you done your lessons? Remember you have a test to prepare.

THEIR SON. Yes, Dad. I've almost finished . . . All that's left is the end of the Restoration.

Sound of a door closing.

HE *(laughs)*. Did you see that? 'Who is "she"? Who is "she"?' repeated firmly and there you have it. He withdrew into his hole. That's what you call putting someone in his place. The place he would never have left if he had had to deal with me. Under lock and key . . . But you, of course . . .

SHE. Naturally, it's well known that I'm always to blame . . .

HE. I didn't force you to say it. But to prove it . . . who said, 'Who is "she"?' Was it you or I? There you were, prostrate . . .

SHE. That's true. Shall I tell you something? I admired you. I admired your courage, your strength . . .

HE. *(chest out)*. Oh, that's going a bit far. I'm normal, that's all . . .

SHE. The fact is that, for a moment, you did weaken, you too were afraid, admit it . . .

HE. Afraid? I? You're dreaming . . .

SHE. But you deserve all the more credit, you know . . . People who aren't afraid . . . But in your case, I saw it; there, when he dared you . . . when you grew angry . . . you had to make a great effort.

HE. Not at all. Not the slightest. I said it, I shouted it, 'It's beautiful. Beautiful. Beautiful . . . '

SHE. Yes, you said it . . . very loudly . . . too loudly . . . there was some thing overwrought, exasperated about it . . . The old carcass was trembling . . . 'But suppose we should fail' . . . And in spite of everything, in spite of hell and high water, you hung on . . . 'Beautiful. Beautiful. Beautiful . . . for dear life . . . It was terrible . . . I felt like stopping my ears, hiding, as far from you as possible . . . I was about disown you . . . When suddenly . . . what made you think of it? Wha presence of mind . . . That was a stroke of genius . . . at such a mome to seize upon that, 'Who is "she"?' Who is "she"?' Marvellous . . . Wl did you find it? It had so completely disappeared. 'Who is "she"?' A have dared to brandish it, to hurl it at him . . . Really, you are wond

HE. I admit that in the pass we had come to . . . or rather he had come to, it had to be done . . . If you had listened to me . . . when it was n yet too late . . . You remember, I said it to you. You remember? . . . tl

30

forbidden words? Words we didn't have the right to use? . . .
In fact, I must say that I myself . . . Lord, how silly we were . . .

SHE. Oh, I'm not so sure . . . Even now, some of those words . . . I couldn't . . .

HE. Yes, now . . . you remember when he was still a puling, damp, wrinkled infant . . . For the life of you, you couldn't, you would never have dared to say . . .

SHE. Yes. To say to anybody, even to him: 'dearie'. Or worse still: 'young man' . . . That's true, that shocked me. It seemed to me that it was sort of like saying . . . like saying, 'kike'. Like saying, 'nigger'. Or 'women-folk'. Impossible. No question of it. There had to be perfect equality . . .

HE. Perfect equality, that's a good one! Equality . . . You're joking. You should say, superiority . . . He was superior to us . . . Entirely composed of exquisite potentialities, of possibilities too numerous to choose from. He was still intact. Before the fall. The falls . . .

SHE *(sighing)*. Yes, before we had made everything impossible, spoiled everything . . .

HE *(ironically)*. We? Not so. Not I. It was not I who wrapped him up the way you do a parcel. It was not I who neglected to talk to him or tickle or kiss him enough while I was changing him . . . Not I who made him wait for his feeds . . .

SHE. Oh, that's not true, I always hurried . . .

HE *(in an awful voice)*. Don't deny it. How many times I used to hear him bawling himself hoarse . . .

SHE *(upset)*. Not for that reason . . .

HE *(bantering)*. Indeed . . . Not for that reason. And when her ladyship tore herself away from those exhilarating conversations . . .
It was too late . . . frustration . . . With all its consequences . . .
Madame may consider herself fortunate. But that's nothing. We can say that we had a narrow escape . . . We had luck. 'A break' . . . as he says . . .

SHE. Yes. That's true. Lots of luck. Just the thought of what could have happened to us . . .

HE. You mean there were worse things still? More serious crimes? . . .

SHE. Oh, no . . .

HE. There were too. Say it. For a long time I've felt that you were hiding something from me. Admit it. It'll do you good. And me too. It will help me to understand your permissiveness . . . to be less exasperated by it . . .

SHE *(firmly, taking herself in hand)*. No . . . It's nothing . . .

HE. Go on, try. You'll see, you'll feel better. It must not be so awful . . . Look, I'll help you . . . You wanted to teach him to be clean? You put him on the pottie . . . you made a sort of whistlin noise . . .

SHE *(horrified)*. Certainly not! What will you invent next? You reme perfectly . . .

HE. That's true, I do remember . . . Perhaps, you took out of his mou . . . while he was asleep . . .

SHE. His thumb? Why, you're crazy. You know perfectly that I never . . .

HE. Well, what then? Darling. Don't torture me. Say it . . . let's share the burden of it . . . Tell me, what is it?

SHE *(in a whisper)*. Once, before he was born . . .

HE. Oh . . . before he was born . . .

SHE *(feverishly)*. But it's known now that that matters. People have told me that. People who know. I've read it. It's been scientifically demonstrated. Everything can go back to that . . . all the mistakes . . . criminal mistakes . . .

HE. Which mistakes? What did you do?

SHE. Oh, it's too awful . . . when I was pregnant . . .

HE. When? In what month?

SHE. It was at the very beginning . . .

HE. At the very beginning . . . let's not exaggerate . . . . That's certain less serious, all the same . . .

SHE. No, apparently it isn't. Some people say it can be even more serious before . . .

HE *(firmly)*. Certainly not. I don't believe that.

SHE. Well, no matter. In any case, it was when he already 'existed' in an embryonic state . . . One day . . . I had . . .

HE. You had what?

SHE. I'll never forgive myself . It came over me all of a sudden. A terrible thought . . . All of a sudden. Oh, it's awful; I didn't want him.

HE. Oh, merely the thought . . .

SHE. Not merely. Not just a thought that quickly flashes across your mind . . . And even that, how can we know what effect . . . But I even . . . . . . *(pauses)* . . . went so far as to cry . . .

HE. oh!

SHE. Yes. Real tears. That rolled down my cheeks. Imagine! The disturbance for him. The shock . . .

HE. How awful! All that play-acting . . . when I think of it . . . your ecstasy when you felt him move . . . that beatific look . . . All pretence!

SHE. Oh, no, don't say that. It was *genuine.* I was happy, happy, happy, happy! There was just suddenly, I don't know how it happened . . . that awful moment . . . Every time I think back on it . . .

HE *(coldly).* In any case, what good does it do? It's better forgotten. What's done is done. You can't change it now. He's there. Just as he is. Shut up, under lock and key. Obtuse. *(Becoming more and more enraged).* — Narrow minded. 'Practical.' Oh, he's no 'dreamer'. No 'esthete': no danger of that . . . comics . . . detective stories . . . juke-boxes . . . sporting matches . . . a fine product. Bravo! we've reached the point, when he's present, of not being able to say 'It's beautiful . . . ' we don't dare listen to a record . . . we're afraid . . . and we have to put up with it. Shall I tell you something? There's only one way . . .

SHE. No. Not that. That would be useless. You know perfectly well that we wouldn't succeed . . . You would be the one to run and bring him back . . . and everything would start over again . . .

HE. Never, you hear me. Never! Let him go to the other end of the earth. They can put him in prison . . . In a reform school. Just so he disappears . . . And to Hell with him.

Pause.

SHE. Oh, after all . . . if you think about it . . . that's going a bit far . . . To have to bear that: just so he disappears! . . . Well, . . . That's how it is . . . You can believe me or not, as you want . . . That's what we've come to!

HE. What did you say? To whom are you speaking?

SHE. Be quiet . . . Yes: 'Just so he disappears. And to hell with him' *(In a voice that is not hers).* Why? What has he done? Is he a murderer? *(In her own voice).* Oh no . . . He wouldn't hurt a fly. *(Different voice).* He's a thief? *Her voice* — Oh, no . . . honesty itself . . . *(Different voice).* A liar? *(her voice).* No. *(Different voice).* A pervert? *(Her voice).* No. No. *(Different voice).* A feignant? . . . [1]

HE. What did you say? I heard *'feignant'.* You didn't say that?

SHE. *(Defiantly).* I did. I did say it. *'Feignant'.* And why not?

HE. My poor darling . . . You must really be suffering . . . So you've come to this . . . That little good-for-nothing has brought you to this . . . has made you demean . . . lower yourself . . . degrade yourself . . . cheapen yourself . . .

SHE. Quiet. A little modesty, I beg of you, A little humility. When people come here for a consultation, they must leave their pretentions outside . . . I did say *'feignant'.* You see, ladies and gentlemen, that's the whole point. He can't bear such words as that. *'Feignant'* is forbidden . . .

VOICES. *Feignant?* Forbidden?

SHE. Yes : . . . You understand? *Fai-né-ant*. That's allowed. That's
superior. Airy. Lofty. *Fai-né-ant*. That's 'beautiful'! While
feignant is ugly. *Fai-né-ant* is beautiful! Beautiful. Beautiful. That's
the whole point. . . . You never know how far that can go . . . His
contempt and his tyranny. And when the poor child can't stand
it any longer . . . When he turns from us . . . his own father goes
as far as to wish . . . Oh, help me . . .

VOICES. If it isn't a shame, to see a thing like that. If that isn't
a shame . . . To want to banish that poor child . . . to come to that.
You could understand if he were wild . . .

SHE. No, indeed, that's not the case.

VOICES. You could understand if he were a crook, or a murderer.

SHE. No.

VOICES. Let's suppose he took drugs . . .

SHE. Not so.

VOICES. Or you could understand if he had the misfortune . . .
You'd understand if he were an ungrateful son . . .

SHE. Not so.

VOICES. Or suppose you were old . . .

SHE. No.

VOICES. Or suppose you were without means and he refused to pay
for your food . . . a thing one sees so often these days . . .

HE. How much longer will that go on? That's enough . . . I can't
bear any more. Stop . . .

SHE *(very softly)*. Watch out, what are you doing? Be quiet. And above
all, don't interrupt. It has to unreel. Be patient. You'll see . . .

HE. I can't, it's more than I can bear. It gives me the staggers, it
nauseates me . . .

SHE *(whispers)*. Do be quiet. *(Aloud)*. Continue, pay no attention . .
You see, he's so refined . . . Very exacting. Always so impatient.

VOICES. If it isn't a shame to see that. Let's suppose he were
dishonest . . .

SHE. No.

VOICES. Let's suppose he were licentious.

SHE. No, No.

VOICES. Let's suppose he were a *feignant* . . .

HE. Oh . . .

SHE. No. He's not a *feignant*. He works . . .

VOICES. If that's not a shame. Not licentious. Not a thief. Not a
liar. Not dishonest. Not a drug-addict. Not *feignant*. There are
lots of people in your place who would be satisfied. Some who
would be proud. And some who would be downright happy. There
are some who never hoped for that much . . . Imagine, in times
like these . . . with the young people you see nowadays . . . with all
those good-for-nothings . . .

HE. Oh . . . that's enough. Enough. I give in. I quit . . .

34

SHE. You're impossible. Wait. And above all, don't rush things . . . You'll see . . . It's coming . . .

VOICES. When you think that some people have such luck. . . A polite boy . . . A conscientious boy . . . A hard-working boy . . .

SHE. Oh yes, he's even in advance for his age.

VOICES. If that's not shameful. They must be spoilt . . . They must be rotten spoilt . . .

SHE *(ecstatic)*. Oh yes, isn't that true?

VOICES. Hard-working . . .

SHE. That he is . . .

VOICES. Do you hear that? . . . When I think of all the people who would give almost anything . . .

SHE. Yes. From that standpoint . . . eh? You'll admit.

HE. Yes, as regards his studies . . . that's true.

VOICES. His studies! . . . You'd think they didn't count . . .

HE. On the contrary . Of course they count . . .

VOICES. Well, then, what's wrong?

HE. *(hesitant)*. It's . . .

VOICES. What?

HE *(mild, softening)*. Oh, it's nothing . . . nothing . . . That's true. Nothing to speak of. Nothing to be anxious about. Nothing to send you looking for trouble. Nothing to make a fuss about . . . We're the ones . . . we . . . we are spoilt . . . Rotten-spoilt . . . We are crazy.

SHE. There, you see, darling.

VOICES. Be careful lest Heaven should punish you. If it should happen . . . May God forbid, let's touch wood . . . Whenever you thought back on it . . .

SHE and HE. Oh yes, may God forbid . . .

VOICES. Oh, you see . . . you're tempting fate . . .

SHE and HE. Oh no.

VOICES. You don't know how fortunate you are . . .

SHE. Oh, yes we do . . .

VOICES. Of course . . . no need to say it. In reality, you're very proud, aren't you? You wouldn't exchange him for anybody, would you? Admit it. A strapping boy like that.

SHE and HE. That's true.

VOICES. Tall, well-built. Sturdy.

HE. Oh, in that respect . . . I feel like a whipper-snapper beside him.

VOICES. And already interested, I bet . . . it's not surprising . . . all the girls . . .

HE. For that matter, there are some already . . . They swarm about him . . . The other day the telephone rang . . . I picked up the receiver and I heard . . .

35

SHE. But he would never do anything wrong. When his father spoke
to him about it, to warn him . . . He interrupted him. He's very
modest you know. With that serious look of his he said: Yes, I agree
with you, I know, Dad.

HE. I myself at that age, was a fool . . . Slightly retarded . . . Always
with my nose in a book . . . Or in museums . . . But he . . . Oh, for h
that's certainly true, such things as that bore him . . . he doesn't like
them . . . what he wants are comic strips . . . television . . .

VOICES. After all, he belongs to his time . . . that's normal, he's like
everybody else . . .

HE *(anxious)*. Everybody else?

SHE. Oh. You're not going to start again? You're not going to have
another attack? . . . *(Loudly)*. Yes. He's like everybody else. Today
everybody his age is like him. Don't make that face, I beg of you . .
Don't bristle up like that. Come on, repeat after me: 'Everybody' . . .
Practise it . . . You'll see, it'll go better . . . Repeat: 'Everybody
does it. Everybody says it. All young people are like that. We are lik
everybody else . . . '

HE *(in a weak voice)*. Everybody does it . . . all young people . . .

SHE. All young people prefer the comics.

HE. All . . . young people prefer . . .

SHE *(severely)*. Come on! . . . the comics.

HE. The comics.

SHE. Juke-boxes. Pin-ball machines.

HE. Juke . . . Yet there are some . . . even among the young people . .

VOICES. Oh, my poor friend, you're talking about exceptions. They
only confirm . . .

SHE. Why, of course. All you need to do is look about you . . . even
among the most brilliant specimens: graduates of the very best
universities . . . the Aubry boys, or the Jamets . . . And yet, it's as
I tell you . . . 'The Wizard of Oz'. 'Lucky Luke', 'Asterix', are their
favourite reading. Their father . . . who would have the right to
demand more of them . . . oh, he just laughed, he thought that
was alright . . .

Pause

HE *(firmly)*. It's finished. Ended. Thumbs down. I don't want to
play any longer.

SHE. What's the matter with you?

HE. What's the matter with me is that you have made a mistake. A
fatal mistake.

SHE. What mistake? with him again? Diapers again? Bottles?

HE. No, a mistake, here and now, with me. You did. You changed
games. Without letting on. But I saw it. You had to drag in old

man Jamet. And the Aubry boys. Now I am going to ask you to let me have Mrs. Dennison, . . . and Mr. Dennison . . . Absolutely, I want both the father and the mother . . .

SHE. What?

HE. Yes, give them to me. Come on, give them here. And now, the daughter and the son. Yes, Dennison. The entire family.

SHE. What will you do with them?

HE. You'll see. I need them. And the Herberts as well. All of them, father, mother, son, grandson. Give them here. And the Charrats. The entire family. I could ask you for others . . . but for the time being, they will be enough for me.

SHE. I don't understand a thing . . .

HE. Wait, you'll understand. Now let yourself go. Repeat after me: say, 'It's beautiful'.

SHE. Oh, what for?

HE. Repeat it, I tell you. I myself was very patient a while ago. Repeat after me: 'it's beautiful'.

SHE. *(wearily)*. 'It's beautiful'.

HE. Repeat: 'It's beautiful are words that we do not dare to use in the presence of our own child.' And now you're going to see, screw up your courage.

SHE. It's beautiful are words that we do not dare to use in the presence of our own child. And now you're going to see . . . '

HE. No, not that . . . not 'and now you're going to see', that was spoken to you.

SHE. And all the rest was spoken to whom?

HE. To the Dennisons, the Herberts, and the Charrats . . .

SHE. Oh listen, how silly we must look! They're going to think we're completely mad.

HE *(nostalgically)*. Mad . . . *(Sighing)*. Fit to be tied. If only you were right. If only it were possible . . . Personally, that's all I ask. Unfortunately, there's little chance . . . Come, brace up. Let's repeat it. But just a second, so I can gather my strength . . . There, I'm ready. Let's start.

SHE and HE. 'It's beautiful' are words that we do not dare to use in the presence of our child . . .

HE. You understand? The words 'It's beautiful' don't come out. *(Aside)*. Oh, God, spare me, I haven't the heart . . . *(Becoming firmer.)* Yes, you see . . . 'It's beautiful', when said in his presence, makes us tremble, makes us panicky . . . There we have it. I've said it . . . now, in a second, the Dennisons, the Charrats . . .

SHE. What will the Dennisons and the Charrats, who are perfectly healthy, normal people, take us for? They've never seen such madness, have they?

HE.   No, darling. You know perfectly that they haven't. Let's
not have any illusions . . . Take your courage in both hands.
The shock will be great. Worse than anything I imagined.
Anything I might have feared . . .

SHE.   What is it? You're killing me . . .

HE.   It's frightful. In a twinkling. In a split second. Right away.
Without hesitating. As though it were the most natural, the
most commonplace thing, they understood . . . Not the
slightest surprise. With a pitying look: *(imitating someone's voice)*.
'Oh how sad that is . . . It's really a great misfortune . . . People
before whom one doesn't dare to say 'It's beautiful'.

MRS DENNISON'S VOICE.   I flee them like the plague . . . But then,
when it's a question of your own child . . .

MR. DENNISON'S VOICE.   It's a misfortune . . .

HE *(toneless voice)*. You think so?

THE DENNISON and OTHER VOICES.   Of course we think so.

HE.   But why, really, why? I never have quite understood . . . I
tell myself that I'm mad. Explain it to me . . .

VOICES.   Explain it to you? What's the use? Why turn the knife in
the wound?

HE.   Do, I beg of you, do turn it. I want to know. It's perhaps not
for the same reasons, that you and I . . . We may not be thinking
about the same things . . .

VOICES.   Alas, we are, my poor friend, what else do you expect us
to be thinking about? Shall we tell you?

HE.   Yes, do. Tell it . . .

VARIOUS VOICES.   You must really be in a very bad way . . . you're
in a panic, you're afraid, because you sense an insulting barrier . . . a
vile contempt . . . a furtive threat . . . which those people cause to
weigh on everything that matters, they debase and level everything,
everything that makes life worth while . . . *(Becoming excited)*. You
ashamed before them of profaning . . . you feel you want to withdra
from their contact . . . to put things in safe keeping . . . above all,
they must not be provoked . . . they must not come too close . . .
in fact, just to think about it . . . horrors . . . why talk about that?
Nobody mentions it out of embarrassment . . . or out of just plain
decency . . . But who doesn't feel that?

SHE.   Who? Why, most people. Healthy people. Normal. Strong.
whose heads are well screwed on their shoulders. Their hearts in
the right place. Thank God there are some people like that. Adults.
Hardened. Whom life had confronted . . . to whom it has taught
something more than the refinements of this spoilt, dissolute,
rotten lot . . . A threat? Bad luck . . . a misfortune . . . to have
had him . . . to have a son like him . . . But it's almost unbelieveable
(Imitation). Is he a murderer? Of course not. *(Imitation)*. A thief?

A liar? No. *(Imitation)*. A pervert? No. *(Imitation)*. A feignant?
. . . *(Weeps.)*

THE DENNISON'S VOICES.   Ah, my poor friends, so you've come
to this . . . Asking for help . . . going to consult healers, bone-
setters . . . writing letters to the agony columnists . . . Who could
throw the first stone at you? . . . In desperate cases, what will
one not do? We ourselves if, by ill luck, such a thing had
happened to us with Jack or Peter . . . They, thank heaven, up
till now, are always poking about . . . as soon as they have a free
moment . . .

HE *(avid)*.   Yes, isn't that so? In books? Museums? At all the exhibi-
tions? Good records . . . Art books. Yes, the way I used to be . . .
But you know, at times, I wonder . . . I don't mean to offend you . . .

VOICES.   What is it? What is it you wonder?

He.   Well, if there wasn't perhaps in that, a certain something that
was lacking . . . yes . . . a certain vitality . . . Our son, you know,
a stalwart fellow. Bursting with health and youthful strength.
Not a little old man the way I was at that age. He's got a good
head. A strapping physique. Already interested , , , he is that . . .
(laughter) quite a heart-breaker. *(Chuckles)*. Of course we ourselves never mix in . . . Besides, he has already reached a stage of
maturity . . . that is astonishing for his age . . .

SHE.   A very open mind. He never lets himself be taken in . . . No
authoritative arguments go with him. He sifts everything through
a fine sieve.

VOICES.   Well, then, what are you complaining about? What is it that
makes you suffer? Everything's fine. You can be satisfied. Proud.
Let's all be happy in our way.

HE *(worthy)*.   Yes, you're right. We were wrong.

SHE.   Excuse us. Yes. Let's all be lucky in our way.

Silence

HE.   Did you hear that pitying tone . . . As though they were speaking
to feeble-minded people . . .

SHE.   Yes. But admit it was coming to us. Just imagine! And you re-
proached me with lowering myself! You can say that you baited
them . . . *(imitating them.)* I do feel sorry for you . . . such a de-
meaning contact . . . one would like to hide everything . . . everything that 'matters' . . . simple decency – shame on you – keeps
people from talking about those things . . . How awful if such a
misfortune . . . if that had happened to us . . . if our Jack or our
Peter . . . But in front of them *(gradually changing her tone)* no
danger, in front of them, we can say 'It's beautiful'. We can swoon.
Kneel down . . . All together. The whole family. Bow our heads
at the same time . . . There's no danger that they would raise
theirs . . . No, quite so. No danger. Not like in our family . . .

Come in, darling, come on in here with us . . .

What have you been doing? Did I interrupt you? Come in, do, just for a minute . . .

THE SON. Yes, mama. What's the matter?

SHE. Well, darling, I just wanted to ask you . . .

THE SON *(a bit excited)*. Yes, I've finished. All I have to do now is to make a summary . . .

SHE. No, no, that's not what I wanted to speak to you about . . .

THE SON. Well, then . . . What was it?

SHE. Don't look like that . . .

THE SON. Like what?

SHE. Don't make that baby-face.

HE. Oh, you do have some good ones! What do you expect? Do you think you have a magic wand that can transform the swan into Prince Charming, or the frog into a beautiful princess? You know quite well that I put a spell on him.

SHE *(to her son)*. Do you understand what your father's saying?

THE SON. No, mama.

SHE *(begging)*. Of course you understand . . . You're pretending you're stupid . . .

THE SON. Certainly not . . . Really . . .

HE. You may be sure that now, no matter how you try . . . I told you that before, I put him in his place . . . I locked him in. Who's 'she'? You thought that was fine. You admired my presence of mind, my courage . . . Now you'd like him to come out. You have to decide what you want. Would you like for him to begin again?

THE SON *(with a naive expression)*. For me to begin what again?

SHE. Why, darling, you know perfectly . . . I would like for you to be again the way you were a little while ago . . . when you understood everything better than we did, when you sensed everything so clearly . . . we were the ones who were like children . . . when you yourself said, you remember, that we didn't dare to utter . . . to say: 'It's beautiful' . . . simply because you . . . because you were present . . . You are so sensitive, so keen . . . All those things, for you too, when you feel like it . . . nothing can be hidden from you, it's impossible to astonish you . . . you have such clear-sightedness, such a free mind . . . I wish the same for the people . . ..

THE SON. But you were so frightened. And dad was furious . . .

SHE. That was ridiculous. I'm sure he realizes it now . . . he should have let you explain yourself, assert yourself . . . And he, with his 'Who's she?', that was not intended to crush you, you know . . . I know him . . . he couldn't help it . . . a simple reflex . . . 'who's she'? . . . out of habit. Out of conformity. So old-fashioned. 'Who's she?' I ask you, after all, Such trifles . . . Where did he get that . . . when we were there, all three of us, in one of those rare moments when finally . . . it's marvellous . . . all of a sudden . . . it's like a rift in a cloud . . . We were finally about to experience something . . . between ourselves . . .

HE. Oh listen, stop. Don't you think you've had enough? You want more? . . . You have only yourself to blame . . . I warn you. Don't expect me to come to your rescue . . .

SHE. *(uplifted).* No, no, I'm not counting on it . . . I won't need it . . . *(to the son).* Listen, darling, I beg of you, tell me, tell me . . . don't refuse . . . tell me . . . just why . . . why, do you think, tell me . . . when you are present, even on the other side of the wall . . . as you expressed it so well . . . we can't . . .

THE SON *(airily. Very much at ease).* Ah, that, it's true, you see yourself, even now, in the midst of all these effusions, you stop, you don't dare . . .

SHE. *(taking herself in hand).* But I do dare, you see: 'It's beautiful'. And I'll even show you. I'll drag it out . . . look, watch me, before you. And I'll say — do you hear me? 'It's beautiful . . . ' And I'll ask you, you too: Don't you think so?

Silence

. . . Well, say something!

THE SON. Well, there's nothing to be done about it . . . I can't help it . . . I cringe. In a moment *(in a jokingly terrible voice).* I'm going to secrete, the way an octopus does . . . black ink will spread over everything . . . Look at dad, he's already all doubled up . . .

HE and SHE. *(toneless voices).* Don't you think that's beautiful? You hate that? . . . all that . . .

THE SON. *(condescendingly).* No, of course not . . . that's not the question . . .

HE and SHE *(with hope).* Not the question . . . Oh, darling, what is it then?

THE SON. It's . . . It's . . . but it embarrasses me to say it to you . . . It's going to shock you.

SHE. No, no, I beg of you, say it . . .

THE SON *(hesitant).* Well, it's that expression: 'It's beautiful' . . . that ruins everything for me . . . it's enough for that to be plastered on anything whatsoever, and right away . . . everything seems like . . .

SHE. Yes . . . I believe I see . . .

THE SON. Yes . . . you do see . . .

SHE. I understand . . . it becomes conventional . . . doesn't it?

THE SON. Yes, I suppose so . . . Commonplaces of that kinds, as soon as you apply them . . .

HE and SHE *(full of hope).* Yes. One shouldn't, you're right. It's a sort of facility. Conformity.

41

THE SON.   Yes, that's it . . . I have a horror of . . .

SHE *(aroused).*   Yes , you, you have too much respect for things like that . . .

THE SON *(irritated).*   Ah, there we are. Now it's respect. Always those words.

SHE *(humble).*   Excuse me . . . I meant to say that the thing itself . . . on which we plaster the words . . . and which you don't want to see flattened out, isn't that so?, or banalized . . . but the thing itself, it . . . you . . . you . . . after all . . .

THE SON.   Why yes, mama, of course . . .

SHE *(to the father).*   You see how mistaken we were. How little we knew our own child . . . That's true, they are the ones we know least well . . . He doesn't at all hate . . . He likes, you see . . . well, 'likes' is an unsuitable word . . . forgive me . . . we are so awkward . . . oh, well . . . I mean to say that what your father was showing me a while ago, this engraving . . . you, too, if you would look at it without anybody saying a thing, you too . . .

THE SON *(reassuring).*   Why yes, I too, of course . . .

HE.   You too? Eh? You think so? You don't think that it's . . .

SHE *(panicky).*   Oh no, stop, be careful . . . don't begin again . . . not those words . . . which are so conventional . . . sclerotic . . . emphati . . . you see, darling, I believe that I understand . . .

HE.   Alright, alright, granted . . . since he's so refined . . . *(delighted)* so delicate . . . But after all, it's, isn't it? . . . don't you think so? . . .

Whistle

THE SON.   Yes. It's pretty nifty, that I'll grant you.

HE *(delighted).*   Nifty. Nifty. Nifty. I shouldn't have thought of that. Nifty. Now I'll know. One word is enough! . . .

SHE *(feverish).*   Yes, for everything to change . . . for real understandi for it to be possible yes, isn't that so?

HE.   Watch out. You get carried away every time. . .

SHE.   That's not so, I'm not carried away . . . *(Feverishly, as though about to explode and pour forth).*   Listen, darling, I've always know this, always felt it, we are so like each other . . . It wasn't possible . . now, isn't it so? I can say it to you, share . . . you remember? like in the old days . . . when you were little . . . when you yourself came t show me . . . now we'll go . . . we won't? that doesn't tempt you? You'd rather go all by yourself . . .

THE SON.   Go where?

SHE.   Why, you know, I spoke about it the other day . . . something . no, don't worry, I am careful . . . something that should not be missed, you'll allow me to say that . . . for me it was a shock . . . an event . . . that exhibit . . . But perhaps you have already seen it? . . .

42

No? very well, it's not that . . . What's the meaning of all this
supervision? . . . very well, let's leave it . . . but I'd like to
show you . . . look . . . no not at that . . . not reproductions . . .
(coaxing).   You'll see, be patient . . . or rather you'll hear . . .
. . .

A few measures of Boucourechliev.

No . . .
HE *(Whispers).*   You're crazy . . .
SHE.   Yes, that's not it . . . wait . . .

A few measures of Webern.

No, not that either . . . But I know what . . . I think that this
time . . .

Mozart, for longer.

HE.   Oh, that'll do. *(He turns off the record.)*
SHE *(tearful).*   But why did you do that? We were listening so
   intently . . . It penetrated . . . it filled everything . . . it was . . .
HE.   Nothing. It bores me stiff.
SHE.   It bores you stiff?
HE.   Yes. I think it's boring . . .
SHE.   You do? You don't think that it's . . .
HE.   That it's what?
SHE.   That it's . . . well, pretty nifty . . .

Silence

But what's happening?
HE.   What's happening is that that bores me . . . What's happening is
   that I don't want . . . now now.
SHE. *(weeping).*   Oh . . .
HE.   Not as long as he's here . . . it doesn't penetrate . . . I cease to
   hear anything. I don't feel anything . . . everything is shrouded in
   black ink . . . Quick, help! . . . help me, please . . .
THE SON *(very calm and a bit condescending).*   Alright, oh, alright.
   I'll go. Calm down a bit . . . It's not about all that, but a while ago
   Mr. Bertrand called. I answered . . . He'll call back . . .
HE *(relieved).*   At what time?
THE SON.   I said you'd be home after eight o'clock . . .
HE.   Why eight o'clock? . . . When I had said that I would be back at
   the latest . . .
THE SON.   Excuse me, you didn't say it to me . . .
SHE.   No, you said it to me . . .
HE.   No, to him.
SHE.   No, to me.
THE SON.   So you see.

43

HE.   In your defence, your mother would say anything . . .

THE SON.   No. You know perfectly well that she never lies.

HE.   Are you giving me a lesson? And besides, who are you talking about? Who is 'she'?

[1] Footnote p. 33: Readers and actors will want to use their own term for *feignant* (an uncultured pronounciation for *fainéant*). 'Good for nothin' ', 'scrounger' or 'lazybones' are among the possibilities, although the latter does not convey the sense of a slip into an uncultured pronounciation.

Izzum
or What is called nothing

Translated by Maria Jolas

Isma (Izzum) was first performed at L'Espace Pierre Cardin in February 1973, with the following cast:

HE	Michel Lonsdale
SHE	Dominique Blanchard
MAN 1	François Darbon
MAN 2	Gérard Depardieu
MAN 3	Michel Robin
WOMAN 1	Nicole Hisse
WOMAN 2	Pascale de Boysson
WOMAN 3	Tatiana Moukhine

Directed by Claude Régy

HE.   Disparagement? Dis-par-age-ment. Yes, that's it: disparagement.
What we've just been indulging in was disparagement. You could
also have called it slander. Or backbiting. But you chose
disparagement. I understand. To tell the truth, I was expecting
it. You too were expecting it, weren't you? We were both expecting
it. Had been for some time . . .

SHE.   Yes . . . I saw it coming. Things were going too well . . .

HE *(sighs)*.   There's nothing we can do about it. Nothing left but to
give in. Nobody can resist that. You see how uncomfortable everybody looks? That they certainly do. They would like to hide under
the carpet. Their embarrassment could have restrained you.
That happens, doesn't it? that the embarrassment we're about to
cause others . . . embarrasses us, so much so that we prefer to endure
. . . Oh well, I express myself badly, but you understand what I
mean: one sees things like that every day.

SHE.   To be frank, I was more or less counting on it. But it just so
happens that it did not embarrass you . . .

HE.   It didn't? Really? Not even a little?

M 1.   Less in any case than listening to such disparaging remarks . . .
That's really more than I can bear.

W 2.   I'm like you, I must admit . . . in such cases, I always say to
myself what a knocking I must get when my back is turned.

HE.   You see; she's coming to herself again. You waked us up.
Now we can see. It's funny the way, all of a sudden, everything
has reassumed a familiar, normal aspect . . . A bit insipid . . . Not
even? Not insipid?

M 1.   No. For me, in fact, this kind of titillation . . . Well, I thought
it was rather stultifying.

W 2.   There we were tearing into shreds . . . those poor Dubuits . . . .
They really don't deserve all that.

M 1.   Then let's forget them, for Heavens sake, let's look for
another subject of conversation.

HE.   Yes. Let's do. I'm quite ready, you know I too can become
easily interested in a lot of things.

W 3.   Just so we don't continue to look at one another the way
we're doing . . .

HE.   Oh, let's not exaggerate. We wanted to have a bit of fun, to
shine, enhance our image, give vent to our aggressiveness, our

guilt feelings . . . tickle one another, scratch one another . . . melt together, separate . . . kill, devour, exorcise one another . . . I don't have to enumerate everything, it's all too well known. In very current usage, in fact. There's nothing to beat one's breast about. Now it's finished. We've been called to order. Thanks to this gentleman's courage. We shall now exercise our creative powers in a quite dignified manner.

Silence.

HE. Well then! What are we waiting for? It seems to me that we have an unlimited choice of subjects. Let's see, now; let's make an effort.

W 3. The fact is, it's not easy, like that, to order . . .

M 3. Perhaps you would prefer for us to remain silent . . .

W 1. Oh, no, above all not that . . . Above all, now . . .

W 3. No, no, anything rather than that . . .

Silence.

W 1. An angel passed overhead.

W 2. Yes, an angel passed.

HE. Excellent. Just what was needed. Intended for just this type of circumstance. Now, then . . .

VOICES.

Fine.

Wonderful.

Entirely different from his earlier style.

Too bad, I couldn't imagine . . .

Nor could I. I kept putting it off . . . Now it's too late . . .

It's always like that.

The voices then degenerate into background noises from which emerge words, spoken in various ways.

(stressed.) Ra — ving mad . . .

(heavy and dragged out). Personally, you know, in matters of that kind . . .

(dry and determined). It's a question of opinion.

Laughter.

Intolerable.

I quite agree.

You do have some good ones.

48

(whistling and disgusted). Frightful. Not a spark of
inspiration.

(obsequious and avid). Oh yes, I'm like you, I would prefer . . .

Prolonged background noises. Laughter. Little squeals.

M 2. Don't forget, you're the one to give the signal.
W 2. I know, but it's too early. It's not even a quarter after
eleven.
M 2. Watch out, you know quite well that if you keep on
saying it's too early you'll prolong things . . .
HE *(to her, softly).* They can't bear it any longer . . .
M 1. What did you say? They can't bear it any longer?
HE. Of course not, I did not say that . . .
M 1. Yes you did. I heard you.
HE. No, you did not; what I meant to say . . .
SHE. Let's not . . . I beg of you . . . not now . . .
HE *(to her, softly).* Aren't you ashamed! You're a quitter. A
defeatist! *(Out loud).* Do you know what I was thinking
about?
VOICES.

No.

Tell us.

About what?
HE. I don't dare. I'll get another rap on the knuckles.
M 1. If it's still the Dubuits . . . none of that, you hear? You're
not going to start that again?
W 3 *(weary, disappointed tone).* Alright, so it's not the Dubuits . . .
What then?
HE. Don't worry. No more Dubuits. No. However a while back,
this gentleman set me an example.
M 1. I'm flattered. But I don't quite get it. Don't you think,
just the same, that we were indulging, the way we did before in
. . .
HE. Oh no, not that. Besides, it's really not up to me to talk
of disparagement. Although, to tell the truth, there was one
moment . . .
W 3. When we were talking about Valéry?
M 1 *(very dignified).* No connection. To begin with, Valéry
is dead. And above all else, he's a great writer.
W 3. That's the kind of detail that makes all the difference.
W 2. Of course. There's nothing you can say to that . . . Every-
body has a right . . . It's even a duty.
W 1. It's the price of genius.

W 2. That's true. There's no point of comparison. They are
above . . . beyond . . .

HE. I'll acknowledge that the poor Dubuits are not 'beyond'.
They are inside, entirely inside, the way we are . . . That's just
it . . .

M 1. You're not going to start again?

HE. Oh no, as I said. *They* are not the ones concerned.

W 1. *(nostalgically)*. Then who is?

HE. Why, as it happens, nobody.

W 3. *(disappointed)*. So it'll be like it was before?

HE. Certainly not. I'm like this gentleman. I stood it for a
good while, then I did like he did.

M 1. What are you doing like me?

HE. Well, I'm taking my turn at calling everybody to order,I
am making so bold as to express out loud, as you did, my
modest opinion about what is going on.

SHE. Oh, I beg of you, stop. I can't bear it.

HE. I can very well bear it. I think it's beginning to do some good.
We've had enough now, it gets to be exhausting, finally . . . You
don't sense how old-fashioned all that was? a while ago? It was
a copy of a copy, didn't you think so?

M 1. Copy of a copy?

SHE. What he means is that, a while ago, when we were talking,
it seemed to him like an imitation . . . isn't that it?

HE. Yes, I must admit that it beats me . . . After everything we've
been shown, everything we've been shown everywhere . . . in the
theatre, in novels . . . that we should still be able to discuss . . . so
perfectly seriously . . . we ought to feel embarrassed . . .

SHE. That's true, don't you think it's amazing? No matter how often
writers reveal, show us . . . enough to give us a permanent distaste fo
it . . . it's as though they were talking to themselves, we keep on as
if nothing had happened . . .

M 1. That's normal. What's the connection? With them it's art. With
us, it's life. Two separate domains. Nothing in common.

HE. Well, personally *(pretending to be stupid)*, now that I've been
shown that . . . So clearly . . . It can't be helped: I see it everywhere. As soon as people start talking like that, right away, I clamp
it on . . .

M 2. What do you mean by 'it'?

HE. Well, exchanging commonplaces. Stock phrases . . . You know
perfectly. Haven't you heard it said often enough? Hasn't it been
pinpointed enough? Aren't you embarrassed to have let yourselves
fall into that trap again?

W 2. After all. We couldn't do otherwise. We were obliged to 'fill in
the silence' with something.

W 1. And quickly. It was urgent. We had to seize upon whatever was at hand. What was all ready for use, necessarily.

M 1. And what of it . . . I don't understand . . . What are you complaining about? At the theatre you listen to it for hours, it induces a sort of voluptuousness. People remain buried in enormous novels just to watch it unreel page after page.

W 1. Oh, I adore that.

W 2. You recognize yourself. Then you don't recognize yourself.

W 1. That's true. You see yourself . . . without seeing yourself . . . you laugh . . .

M 3. You give a sickly smile . . .

M 2. Yes, but in fun, not really . . . Not really sickly . . . It's delightful.

W 1. That's very familiar. Universally known. At the same time it takes on an unfamiliar aspect, as though it had never been seen before . . .

W 3. A veil is torn . . .

HE. What veil? What's torn? That's not true. It's absolutely not true. Pure fiction. 'Literature' . . . There's nothing true about it.

M 2. Not true? No commonplaces? That's not what we're bandying about?

M 1. Of course it is. And why not? The commonplace is the place where people meet . . .

M 3. Where we share our little stockpile.

SHE *(resigned).* Yes. A real dowry that's been set aside for us ever since we were children . . .

W 3 *(ironic).* Which we dip into when we need to.

SHE *(Sighing).* The way we did a while ago . . .

M 1. Exactly. The way we did a while ago . . . And as for *me*; I thought that was very nice . . . Better, in any case, than your little incursions . . . among the Dubuits . . .

HE. Better? You think so?

M 1. Yes. Better. Clean. Innocent.

SHE. Oh, listen, he's right, don't say he's not, exchanging commonplaces — that's unadulterated, that's pure. Nothing behind it.

W 2. Of course, everybody knows that. It takes place purely on the surface . . . that's what gives commonplaces their charm.

M 3. No, my dear; surface — won't do. Surface implies depth . . . and depth, you know perfectly . . .

W 2. Yes, I know: it's quite out of date.

M 1. It's worn to a shred.

W 1. And yet, at times, I'll admit . . .

HE. You occasionally sense . . . sort of whiffs . . . from down

below? Is that it? Sweet old tunes come back to you? It can't
be helped, isn't that so? No matter how hard you try to
refrain from it . . . A while ago, for instance, to take an example
close to hand, underneath our small talk, what a concert could
have been heard by an attentive ear! Indeed, it's the same with
nearly all commonplaces . . . You have only to choose at random,
any one will do, the most vapid, the most innocent, such as:
What a summer, eh? there are no more seasons! Or this one:
So it goes, time passes. And we're not growing any younger! Or:
I like this book because it's a monument of language . . . and
through that . . . what we could see . . . If we only wanted . . . or
dared . . . But as it happens, you don't want to. Hands off
commonplaces. They are there for that . . . to mask or to smother . . .
Whereas with the Dubuits . . . Well, the Dubuits had this advantage . .

M 1.   No, not that. You promised us.

W 3.   Go on . . . let him do it . . . just a little . . . The Dubuits . . .
all the same, that was . . . I'll admit . . .

HE.   You'll admit that wasn't bad, was it? *(Gluttonously)*. You'll
admit that the Dubuits . . . had something . . .

M 1.   But they're an *idée fixe* with you. An obsession. That can be
treated, you know.

HE.   No, it can't. Too late. Finished. You can't start again. We
gave in once . . .

SHE.   There was nothing else to do. After your outburst . . . That
was a feat.

HE.   A real putsch. But now they've all understood what régime
they were living under . . . Everybody's longing for the Dubuits.

M 1.   Everybody wants to start running people down again! . . .
Wallowing in gossip? . . . you like that? . . .

HE.   You see, that doesn't scare people any more, you can say:
gossip, disparagement, as often as you like. Nobody cares a hoot
any more.

W 2.   I thought that was very impolite, to tell you the truth. They'd
have to shoot me for me to make so bold . . .

M 3.   Me, too . . . as to set myself up, like that, to censure people . . .

HE.   You see. Everybody's against you. I told you so.

M 1 *(indignant)*.   But all of you, a while ago . . .

M 3.   For me, gossip, I can't help it . . . I can never resist it. I
always give in . . . at least at the time . . .

M 2.   Yes, so do I, these reprimands . . . of course, I'm docility
itself, but there's nothing I loathe more.

M 1.   Well, what I myself thought was specially outrageous . . .

HE.   But why argue? Nobody hears you.

SHE.   Nobody believes you.

HE.   But they do, you know. I believe him. I thought he was

playing a game with all that talk of purity and morality . . . but
I've begun to say to myself that I was wrong: the Dubuits do not
interest him. He doesn't give a rap about the Dubuits.

M 1.   That's true. Absolutely. And even — this is going to shock you —
the Dubuits bore me.

SHE.   The Debuits bore you? Oh, that's not possible!

HE.   Oh, yes it is. It's surely true. I know it's hard to believe! It's such
a rare case . . .

M 1.   A rare case! . . . that's a good one . . .

HE *(seriously)*.   Yes, very rare. I'm talking about real cases. Because
there are quantities of make-believe ones. But real cases like yours . . .
well, there are some, of course . . . since great literature . . . since it
interested such geniuses as Dante . . . Dostoyevsky . . .

M 1.   Dante? Dostoyevsky? . . . That's beginning to interest me . . .

HE.   Yes, you know, the lukewarm. The indifferent. The ones that
compose the first circle in Hell, the ones in the Apocalypse . . . It's
a pity to say it, but you are one of them.

SHE.   No, leave him alone, you're digressing . . . It's a waste of time . . .

HE.   Alright, that's that. Listen, to speak quite simply . . . you can take
it or leave it . . . Choose. Who here wants to drop the subject of the
Dubuits? Who would rather take it up again? . . . Who would like
to make a brief return visit to high-minded, authorized subjects?

VOICES.

No.

Oh, no.

Above all, not that.

HE.   You see. They've made their choice. You're outvoted. Even those
who remain silent don't dare . . . You're alone. The only thing left
for you to do now is . . .

M 1.   Precisely. The only thing left for me to do now is to leave. Besides,
I must get up early tomorrow . . . Yvonne, are you coming?

W 1.   . . . No . . . I think . . .

M 1.   Why, what's got in to you?

W 1.   No. I'm sorry, but I'm staying.

HE.   Madam, do you refuse to follow your husband? You know that's
very serious. I shouldn't want, on my account . . .

W 1.   No, I've made my choice. I'm staying.

M 1.   Yvonne, I beg of you, think what you're doing. I can't forgive
you this.

W 1.   You won't forgive me this . . . that's a good one! Listen to him!
He won't forgive me . . . if I refuse to return in a pure, dignified, modest
manner . . . to his diet of milk-toast and oatmeal . . . High-minded
subjects only. Politics. Art. Or only about people who are dead. Famous
people. Gide. Valéry. Vigny. Chateaubriand. Heads in the air,

star-gazing. Not even the right to stoop down and take a whiff, a sniff . . . immediately there's a tap on your shoulder . . . a call to order . . .

M 1. You're disgraceful.

W 1. Disgraceful. I! You know I'm going to tell you something: I have always felt it since the very beginning, but I couldn't put my finger on it. I wanted absolutely . . . for someone to tell me . . . that there's a name for it. And now . . . oh what a relief! He's one of the lukewarm. Indifferent. Amorphous. And Dante! And the Apocalypse! Oh, I didn't ask for all that . . . It's too much. Thanks. Oh yes, I'm staying.

M 1 *leaves. Snatches of good-bye phrases.*

Silence.

W 3. An angel passed overhead.

W 1. Oh, not that. That won't do any more.

SHE. No, I beg of you . . . thank heavens, we've passed that stage . . .

W 3. You're right, excuse me, it was an old reflex.

Silence.

M 2. Yes . . . yes . . . Well, I'll tell you . . . since now one can, quite freely . . .

W 1. Oh yes, tell us . . .

M 2. Well, I have the impression that in any case . . . even without this interruption . . .

W 2. In bad taste . . .

M 2. . . . I have the impression that in any case, we were about to reach our goal.

SHE. Our goal?

M 2. Yes. We were entering the harbour. I was just about to say that you had at hand exactly what you were looking for. Provided for your case. But don't look at me like that . . . I was sure you didn't want to know it. You prefer to torture yourself. You like that.

SHE. Oh, very subtle . . . I'd like to see you in the same situation. Come now, what is it? Don't keep us on tenterhooks.

M 2. An-ti-pa-thy.

SHE *(disappointed).* Antipathy?

M 2. Yes. Precisely, Antipathy. You have an antipathy for the Dubuits. Period. What you sense in the Dubuits . . . a vague inexpressible something . . . that attracts you . . . that fluctuates . . . arouses what is called antipathy. Isn't that what you need? Made to measure. Specially for you. Recognized. Authorized. Perfectly legitimate. Who can say anything against that? Why rack one's brain? Admit that that should keep you quiet.

HE. Antipathy! . . . So that's what you're offering us. We'd be hard to

54

please if we weren't content with that! if we picked at
that! What else do we need?! Who do you think we are?

SHE. See here, my good man, that was the first thing that
came to mind. We thought of that at the start.

HE. Yes, at the very start. When we were trying to calm down.
To stop . . .

SHE. Oh yes, believe me, we really did our best. We even, you
remember, thought we were so mad that we compared
ourselves to that couple of obsessed monomaniacs — Janet
describes them — who, when they lost complete control,
would go down to the cellar, hold hands and rocking back
and forth, repeat in unison: 'One, two, three, we've had enough
phenomena.'

HE. yes: We've had enough phenomena. The Dubuits? So what?
What's the matter? There's something that contains all that.
All of it. Look. Do you see? It's called antipathy . . .

M 2. Then, what more did you need? What was wrong?

SHE. Well . . . no matter how often we repeated it to ourselves
. . . it had no effect. A cauterant on . . . no, it was just the
opposite, not on wood, it kept boiling up just as hard. It hurt.
Saying the word 'antipathy' made no difference whatsoever.

M 2. Is there someone here who can understand that?

SHE. Of course, everybody can understand it. You remember,
in 'The Chalk Circle', the 80-year old married couple? They
came before the judge to ask for a divorce. The judge asked
them 'How long have you been married — Fifty years — so
what's wrong? — Well, we are antipathetic to each other.'
(Laughter). You see, that makes you laugh.

HE. You can see for yourself that antipathy won't do.

W 1. Yes, of course, after fifty years of marriage!

SHE *(avidly)* . . . You can see yourself, antipathy is too vague,
too . . . remote . . . it's just good at the beginning . . . But
afterwards . . .

W 2. That's true. Afterwards, necessarily, people must find
something else.

SHE. Yes, that's so. Oh, poor things, how I understand them . . .
how they must have suffered . . .all their lives . . . imagine
that . . . without succeeding . . .

HE. Exactly like us: Oh, what torture . . .

M 2. So you're cheaters. You're a bad, secretive lot. You want
to be helped and you deceive us. Antipathy won't do . . . The
Dubuits are too close to you, is that it? You've known them
too well? For too long?

M 3. Go ahead, say it: they're relatives?

SHE. Well, yes. The Dubuits . . . are just . . . they're just a cover-up . . . they're a transposition. In reality, it concerns . . . well, it concerns our parents . . . that is to say, my parents-in-law . . . The Dubuits are like them . . .

HE. You're mad, what did you say?

SHE. What do you want me to say, that they're our children?

HE. Why, you're completely out of your head. You forget what that will lead to . . .

SHE. Oh, yes, I don't know what I'm saying. No. Not parents. Not children . . . Oh no . . . For pity's sake. No complexes. No suppressed desires. No infantile fixations . . . Not that: nothing prefabricated. Ready-made. Master-Keys. Frightful mass-produced objects , . . No, forgive me, I lied. *(Silence)*. It concerns our neighbours. We have been meeting them constantly for years. So you understand . . .

M 2. There's nothing you can do about it. Antipathy suits the case very well: neighbours. You meet on the stairs. Good morning. Good-bye. Antipathy can perfectly well justify keeping one's distance . . . There's no need to look for justifications . . .

SHE. You see . . . Neighbours, that won't do. So you're right. It concerns people who are close . . . our brother and sister-in-law. Very kind people. Who have helped us a lot. When we're with them, we like them very much . . . at the time, everything rolls off us, you see; nothing sinks in . . . And then, as soon as they're gone . . . it begins . . .

M 2. It's your older brother?

HE. Oh, no. Above all, not that. I already see what you're leading up to. I see where you are going to take us . . . Not towards that. Not towards the transfer. Not towards jealousy. Not towards inferiority complexes. Good Lord, what were you thinking of? No. We've tried once more to deceive you. The whole truth. Must be told: there's no connection. None. Nothing, precisely . . .

M 3. It concerns whom, then?

SHE. *(pitifully)*. The Dubuits. You know them. That's why we asked you . . . but since antipathy . . . won't do . . . since you didn't want to understand . . . since you had to have justifications . . .

W 1. Listen, there is perhaps something else . . . that you haven't mentioned . . . You're still hiding something from us . . .

W 2. They don't dare say what the Dubuits did to them. Here we are hunting . . .

M 3. Come then, tell us what they did to you, the Dubuits, once and for all. Tell it nicely. Something you don't dare admit. You don't dare . . . publicly . . . Whisper it to me, I won't tell anybody.

SHE. No. They didn't do anything. Anything about which you

could say . . .

W 1.   Well then, something you could not say. Force yourself a bit, if you want to be helped.

SHE.   No. No. There's no question of that . . .

W 1.   What is it, then?

SHE.   It's . . . It's . . .

HE.   It's the fact that they exist.

W 3.   That they exist?

HE.   Yes. There they are. Indestructible. Irreducible.

W 1.   So what? There really is nothing to be in such a state about. If for everything that exists you had to . . .

W 2.   More repugnant things, too — although, to tell the truth, the Dubuits are not repugnant to me. Toads, snakes, rats, yes . . .

M 3.   That's very good. Very soothing. I used to know a man who used this means to get rid of his children . . . They tormented him . . . in the same way . . . they came to haunt him at night . . . they were absurd . . insensitive . . . idiotic . . . he held his head in his hands . . . he told me: I keep saying to myself that *things are like that.* There's nothing you can do about it. That's the way they're made: they exist . . . like monkeys. Like parrots . . . And that relieved him . . . *(Short pause.)* What's the matter? That doesn't suit you, either?

HE.   No, no. Impossible.

SHE.   Absolutely impossible. The Dubuits . . . You could put them through all the metamorphoses, turn them into toads, snakes, rats . . . Or also into beautiful princesses . . . that would not keep . . .

HE.   It would emanate from them in the same way . . .

SHE.   Something that filters from them, that insinuates itself . . . it attacks you . . . it brings out in you . . . it comes through every aspect . . . it comes from nothing . . .

HE *(severe).*   It has its source in them . . . a hidden source . . . it issues from there, it fills us to the brim, it spills over onto everything . . .

Brief silence.

W 3.   Well . . . this will please you . . . I understand you . . . there is, in fact, about the Dubuits . . . *(She whistles slightly).* It's entirely hypocritical. Sweetish. As for her, she coos . . .

W 1.   She doesn't coo. She chirps . . .

M 3.   Granted. Yes. If you like . . . She's very humble . . .

W 1.   A bit childish . . . She pretends to be half-witted.

W 2.   No, why pretends? She is half-witted, believe me.

W 3.   Not half-witted. Slyness itself. She's watching you out of the corner of her eye.

SHE.   Is she? Out of the corner of her eye? Sly?

HE.   Oh, do go on.

W 1 *(in imitation)*. Oh ye-es? Really? And her big eyes open wide . . .

W 2. And that way . . .

SHE. Oh . . . what way?

W 2. I don't know . . .

Silence.

M 3. I know. They try to put themselves within our reach. They stoop to our level . . .

W 2. Yes, that's it, exactly. Only they miscalculate,they stoop too low.

M 3. I used to know Dubuit . . . when, on the contrary, he was trying to climb higher . . . when he was standing on tip-toe . . . on his hind legs . . . in the presence of the powerful and the 'great' . . . He swallowed their disdain, their rebuffs . . . You should have seen that . . . with them he never grew annoyed. But with other people . . . he let nothing pass . . . Enduring rancour . . . I recall that one day, with me, because I had made so bold . . .

W 1. Oh no, excuse me, but that won't do.

M 3. Why not? What's the matter?

W 1 *(turning towards him or towards her)*. Excuse me, you see I wa ready to help you. In a way, I understood you . . . I told you, the Dubuits . . . I too, I have a sort of malaise . . . *(pause. Firmly.)* B go along with this gentleman to the point he wants to take us, exc me . . . that, no, I cannot . . .

M 2. I too, refuse to follow. Don't you?

M 3. What's happening? Another little morality crisis?

M 2. No, oh no . . . but she's right.

M 3. Then I don't understand. They asked me to help them. I made my contribution, which I'll admit was a modest one. But I see tha I was wrong: it was still too generous.

HE. Generous! You dare say that! When you were only acting in your own interest.

M 3. What? In my own interest? What are you talking about?

HE. Yes. Don't pretend to be stupid. You understand me. That got under your skin, didn't it? And you're scratching yourself. In public . . . Shame on you!

SHE. You have satisfied your petty rancour . . .

W 2. It's disgusting. You take advantage of the fact that the Dubui are at your mercy . . . to allow yourself with total impunity . . . t lead us astray . . .

M 3. But you don't like that, do you? It's too crude: I dared too b . . . to reveal . . . what everybody . . .

W 2. Oh, do look at him . . . he's getting mean . . .

M 2. Don't worry: I'm going to clean up all that. And so, my frien you consider that Dubuit has an exacerbated sense of hierarchy?

M 3. Yes, I've always noticed it.

M 2. They 'grovel' in the presence of the 'great'?

M 3 *(more hesitatingly)*. Yes. It seemed to me . . . he ran after . . .

M 2. Is there anyone here who agrees with him? *(Silence.)* Come now, speak up . . . Nobody. I thought so . . .

W 3. That is to say, personally, I must admit, that such distinctions . . .

SHE. That's true for me too, I can't make head nor tail.

HE *(foolishly)*. It's based on what?

M 3. Oh, I don't know . . . Everybody knows it . . .

M 2. Everybody knows it? Not I.

W 1. Nor I.

W 2. Nor I.

M 2. Tell us, it's interesting. It's based on reputation? Money? Influential friends? Tell us . . .

M 3. Oh, that depends . . . I don't know . . .

M 2. Dubuit was obsequious with the people you call 'great'. You said that. Well, who were those great people, I ask you . . . *(Laughter)*. Look this way. Now look that way. Who here is great? Who is small?

M 3. Here! I'm not talking about here.

M 2. But people who have the same sense of hierarchy that you have, see them everywhere.

HE. How about you, yourself.? You are great, that's certain. Which is why — you never suspected it — I'm glad to be your friend. I run after you . . .

M 2. Oh, please . . . Look where that would lead us . . .if like you . . . I blush . . .

W 2. Fortunately, interpretations of that kind, which are annoying . . . it's the least you can call them . . .

W 3. Above all they're so untrue! Based on appearances. On the worst kind of convention.

M 3. To whom were you saying a while ago that Dubuit looked so . . .

M 2. To . . . to . . . It was to Roudier . . .

M 3. Roudier! And yet it was quite clear. There was no need to hunt . . . That's beside the point. Roudier is the full-blooded sort. Heavy drinker. Heavy eater. While Dubuit is the sickly kind. Sort of wizened.

W 1. Yes. It's not surprising that he should have been attracted by Roudier.

W 3. That he should even have been impressed by him . . . in a certain way . . . . why not?

W 1. And also: Dubuit is attracted by people who are anxious.

M 3. Anxious? Roudier? I'd be surprised.

W 3.   Yes, he is. It's true: that frenzied manner. His need for
stimulants: social success, money. That must make Dubuit feel
sorry for him. You know, at bottom, Dubuit is soft-hearted . . .

SHE.   Yes, he is soft-hearted. What you call a heart of gold, isn't
he? That's what we say every time. Enough. Enough of
phenomena. *(Laughter)*. We like him. We like him. Yes, We like him

M 2.   Is that supposed to calm you?

HE.   Oh, yes, that has a calming effect. You're all nice and smooth
inside. As though you'd been ironed. And then afterward, once
more . . . it takes hold of us again . . . we're carried along . . . Oh
no, it can't be helped, you'll never understand. . .

Silence.

W 3 *(shyly)*.   That you'll not deny, that you'll grant, I know . . .
You'll see, you won't feel that you've been affected by it, not the
least demeaned . . . quite the contrary . . .

M 2.   What? What's the matter now?

W 3.   There's no trace of that in me. Nor in any of you. Never. It's
just in them. In the Dubuits . . . something that justifies . . .

SHE.   What, then? Say it.

W 3.   Something certain. Facts. .

SHE.   What facts? Tell us . . .

W 3.   I have this from a reliable source. A young *au pair* girl they
had . . . This can't be invented . . . at night, after she was in
bed, they climbed on chairs and took out . . . from behind piles
of plates . . . they got down on all fours to drag a chest from
under the bed . . .

HE.   A chest? Sounds like Molière. They counted their money?

W 3.   No. Food. Canned goods . . . truffles . . . Chocolates . . . They
guzzled them . . . One night she heard a noise of dishes . . . the
whole pile had fallen . . . jam all over everything . . . they washed
and scrubbed . . . And all that with their stern opinions . . . becau
they preach to other people . . . Oh, it's contemptible *(she is
speaking faster and faster, over-excited, gulping her saliva)* and
people fall for it . . . they listen to them . . . Dubuit, 'soft-hearted
. . . Oh!

SHE.   You see, it's got you. And it hurts. The Dubuits have caught
you.

W 3.   Caught? Me? What have I got to do with it? But to have to
listen to that. Soft-hearted! Oh, that's too much. Hypocrite.
Exploiter. Traitor. And they dare to preach to others . . . . when
they themselves . . . unbeknownst to other people . . . but it
should be shouted from the house-tops, they should be denounced
pilloried.

HE.   Calm yourself. You won't succeed in doing it.

SHE.   Believe me, all you'll do will be to grow more and
    more irritated. It's like biting one's nails . . . pressing . . .
W 3.   Impostors . . . skunks . . .
HE.   Come, come . . . pull yourself together. It's hard, I know,
    when you've let yourself be taken in . . .
W 3.   And you say that to me when you ought to help me.
    So that's your hidden source . . . what you feel . . . it's
    there . . . I've got it . . . behind the piles of plates, in the
    food chest . . . they gorged themselves . . . and they did
    it while everybody around them . . .
HE *(firmly)*.   Control yourself. There. That'll do. You are
    causing yourself pain. Needlessly.
SHE.   These sessions during which we pierce the hearts of
    wax statues — afterwards, how empty it all seems, every
    time, what a disappointment!
W 1.   Yes, a sort of nausea.
W 2.   That's bound to be, what with all those stories of jam
    and pâté de foie gras . . . .
SHE.   We're back just where we started.
M 3.   Really? No pacification?
SHE.   No. None. What people know like that . . . by hearsay
    . . . that adds nothing.
HE.   It came from the outside, you understand. It was furnished
    by others. No connection with what comes from . . . what
    penetrates you . . . what you feel . . . and what, in your case,
    makes you bristle — like fur on a cat's back . . . before you
    can do anything to prevent it . . .
SHE.   Without anything to warrant it . . . And then you'd be
    capable of . . . If it were permitted . . .
HE.   If it implied no punishment.
SHE.   Oh, that's horrible.

Silence.

M 2.   They're right. I understand them. Jam and food chests
    will do them no good.
SHE.   Yes, Yes, that's true. No good. Oh, you do understand . . .
W 3.   Why? It's not true?
M 2.   Oh, no. It probably is true. But they, and try to
    understand this, what they want, is without knowing anything,
    merely from what they sense . . .
SHE.   Yes. From that . . . however insignificant, however tiny . . .
    with that alone . . . to reach the point where . . .
HE.   You can justifiably feel free to . . .
M 3.   Well, it can't be helped . . . I'm going to give it to you. I'm going
    to share with you . . . This time I think you'll be pleased. It's
    exactly what you need . . . It's better than anything you had hoped
    for . . . I'm going to confess that I too . . . the Dubuits . . . I too.

(Whispering, with an air of solemnity). For a long time I've felt . . .

SHE. Oh, you too have felt it?

M 3. Yes. Something awful, terrible.

SHE. Oh, what?

HE. Do be quiet, don't interrupt him.

M 3. They give me the sensation . .

SHE *(avidly).* Yes, don't they? The sensation . . . Caused by what?

M 3. Oh, I don't know . . .

HE. By what? by what? Think!

M 3. By nothing. Nothing you could give a name to.

HE. So what, then?

M 3. It's perhaps . . . No . . . Not even . . . and yet . . . it's perhaps a kind of inner impulsion . . .

SHE. Yes. A sort of wavering. You can see it in her, deep in her eyes . . . there's a little flicker . . .

W 1. Yes, that's true. A cruel little flicker . . . I've seen it too. She has eyes like frosted glass . . . and, at times, it's as though something lighted up behind them . . .

M 3. No, not even that . . .

HE. Just the vibrations of that little laugh of his?

W 2. Yes, I noticed that too. A false little laugh that makes you uncomfortable.

W 1. An icy laugh . . . ha, ha . . . he keeps you at a distance . . .

M 2. That's true. You have the impression that he slams the door in your face.

M 3. No, no, that's much too crude.

SHE. So then . . . but is it possible? You too . . . based on things like that . . . *Izzum . . . Izzum . . .*

HE. Stop, you'll frighten them . . .

SHE *(excited).* Izzum. Izzum. Zum. Zum . . . Capitalizzum. Syndicalizzum. Structuralizzum. That way he has of pronouncing Izzum . . . Turned up at the end . . . insinuating . . . Further. Still further. Right to the heart . . . Like some kind of poison . . . Izzum . . . Izzum . . .

M 2. Ah there, I must stop you. There. There's something too obvious . . . that's self evident . . .

SHE. What is?

M 2. That way of pronouncing words in *ism,* that strikes you, doesn't it?

SHE. Yes. Izzum . . . At the end of words . . .

M 2. And it doesn't make you think of an isthmus?

SHE. Oh, no, never.

M 2. Good. Very good. I understand. You don't like that. You'll see . . . I'm going to get you out of it. Let yourself go. There . . . Don't resist . . . Tell me what associations does that lead to?

W 2. To the isthmus of Panama?

M 2. No, I'm not joking . . . Without thinking about it, tell us what they are.

HE. You see, I warned you. Get out of it if you can.

SHE *(submissive)*. Isthmus . . . yes . . . Narrow . . . Neck . . . Cross . . . Ocean . . .

M 2. Very good. Continue, I think I see.

HE. No. You can't see. That's not the question. Izzum. What matters is the izzum. Obscurantizzum. Romanticizzum. Dubuit has a way of pronouncing that . . .

SHE. Yes. It makes us . . . at times we reach a point where . . . No, of course, you don't understand . . .

M 3. Don't bother. That's not where we are. You're leading us astray. Isthmus or no isthmus, all that is of no use to me. Mere trifles, all that. Flourishes, pretty ornaments. I don't use them.

HE *(dumbfounded)*. Not even things like that?

M 3. No, I need *nothing*. By which I mean nothing. What I sense is based on nothing . . . nothing you could speak of . . . and that has led me . . .

SHE. To what?

M 3. To a crime. A perfect crime.

SHE. A crime? The Dubuits?

M 3 *(whispering)*. Yes. A crime. They committed it perhaps long ago. They perpetrated it in cold blood. One fine day I saw it as clearly as I see you.

HE. But just the same, what allowed you to think?

M 3. Drop the 'allowed'. That kills you. Forget that. I sensed it, and that's that.

W 3. It's a gift, you know. You either have it or you haven't. People who have it, I've known some . . .

W 1. It's a real gift of clairvoyance . . .

M 3. I beg of you, don't pass me off as a clairvoyant . . . with second sight . . . You yourselves can quite well do the same . . . all you need is to break certain habits . . . Pay no more attention to exterior signs . . .

HE. Not the slightest little sign? That's going a bit far.

M 3. No, it isn't. Signs are so misleading. You know perfectly well that actually there are thousands, tens of thousands of murderers . . . they're walking about everywhere . . . and what murderers! they have tortured, degraded, exterminated hundreds of thousands . . . compared to them, the poor Dubuits are little saints . . . and yet, when you look at them, it's a real delight . . . not the slightest waver, not an intonation, not a flicker . . . nothing . . . nothing . . . hearty laughter, clear gaze . . . I won't say more . . . they radiate goodness . . . the real sort . . . they wear their hearts on their sleeves. So, for me, you know, all those signs . . . No. I never took them into account. And then . . . one fine day, it struck me . . .

HE.   But tell me, how do you mean, struck?

M 3.   Struck. It's there. No possible doubt. And I'll tell you better still. At times, I sense that they know I know.

W 2.   That they know?

M 3.   Yes. They know it. But they don't care, you see. They've accepted it once and for all. They have taken this upon themselves deliberately . . . It's an enormous burden that they have agreed to bear. It's there inside them . . . a heavy stone slab.

W 1.   Yes, now . . . it's like the hunter's gun in the tree . . . you know . . . in certain sketches . . . it can't be helped, I see that too. A heavy slab inside them. That weighs a lot!

W 2.   A grave stone!

M 2.   The Dubuits! But that's incredible! That's mad!

M 3.   *(impatiently).* You know, my friend, that, in real life . . .

W 3.   Why of course, certainly, it's not an argument, everybody know it: in life incredible things are hidden everywhere . . . If I told you . . .

W 1.   Don't. Another time. Let's not digress . . . *(To M 3.)* What crime do you think?

M 3.   As for that, I don't know. A real one. That's all.

W 1.   A child . . . the son they had. I've noticed that they never speak of him.

W 2.   That's right. Never a word.

W 3.   Their mother. That struck me . . . after her death.

W 1.   She was a burden to them . . .

HE *(to her).*   Are you not feeling well?

SHE.   Oh, better still . . .

M 3.   Aren't you satisfied?

W 1.   You're not? Why, I thought everybody was feeling in a good mood.

W 2.   Yes. All together. Cosy.

M 2.   All friends. All alike. There was such intimacy . . .

M 3.   Yes, isn't that so? Fusion. Everybody felt the same repulsion, the same horror . . . And it didn't require so much as a shadow . . a batting of the eye . . . not a waver . . . Not an izzum . . . What more could you want, for God's sake?

SHE.   But try to understand me. *(Sighs).* Oh, no, it's too awful, there's nothing to be done about it . . .

M 3.   No. The fact is, I don't understand.

SHE.   Try again, explain it to them . . .

HE.   Well . . . you mentioned flourishes. Ornaments. Flickerings, waverings . . . izzums . . . for you it was that. For us — it's the contrary: izzum is what is essential. *Izzum* is what is important. The crime is just to dress it up . . . something added . . . useless. *Izzum* by itself . . .

SHE. Izzum. With nothing else. Izzum . . . that arouses something in us . . . At times, if only because of that, I could line them up against the wall. Set up gallows . . . Destroy. Exterminate . . . Relentlessly. Pitilessly. And that fills me with anguish, you understand. I have no right. It's shameful.

HE. So we want to erase, forget it . . . We do all in our power, everything . . . We would . . .

SHE. We want to like them, you understand. And when we see them . . . we succeed, we do like them . . . izzum glances off us without penetrating . . . hardly a tickle . . .

HE. And then, as soon as they're no longer there . . . it sinks in. It goes deeper and deeper. It becomes intolerable . . . The mere idea of seeing them again . . .

SHE. I keep hoping and watching . . . sometimes I look through the news items in the papers . . . to see if by chance an accident . . . But no. They're still alive! They're still there. It's there, somewhere, lurking . . .

Brief silence.

W 2. Personally, to tell the truth . . . after listening to all of that! Frankly, for me, it's so much Chinese. Quite sincerely, I just do not understand it. How puritanical! How severe! I feel sorry for you. I, for instance, projecting ears.

SHE. Projecting ears?

W 2. Yes. You heard right; projecting ears. That's all. And that's enough. A necessary and sufficient circumstance.

SHE. Oh! and for that you feel free to detest people.

W 2. Detest? Why such deep sentiments? They're so tiresome. Too much of an honor. Projecting ears . . . *certain* projecting ears . . . I repeat *certain,* because there are all kinds of ears . . . certain ears . . . their shape, I imagine, also plays a role, their color and, as I said before, the angle at which they project; because of all that I eliminate people.

HE. You eliminate? How?

W 2. Oh, within authorized limits, it can't be done otherwise: I keep their owners at a distance. Not even at a distance. I just don't *see* them. As though they had ceased to exist. Why stand for that if it's painful to me?

W 3. When you think about it, that's true. Ears, toes . . . toes too sometimes have an effect that is . . .

W 1. Yes. Radical!

SHE. And if you're obliged to?

W 2. Obliged? How do you mean?

SHE. Suppose you're in the same compartment, or in the same office? If it's a person in the next bed to yours in a hospital ward? If you share the same prison cell?

W 2. I manage. My eye alights somewhere without seeing them.

M 2. Yes. That's true. Everybody does that. Beyond the range of the lens. Banished. Eliminated.

HE. The entire person?

W 1. Oh, you know . . . when a person's ears or toes have that effect, there must be something . . .

W 2. Probably. But I don't waste my time looking. Why complicate life? I banish such people and that's that. I eliminate them, as far as I'm concerned. Enthusiasts can no doubt be found elsewhere . . . there are always some . . .

SHE. And that doesn't embarrass you?

W 2. Embarrass me? Why on earth should it? You know I'm not the arguing, brainy kind . . . I'm a creature of instinct . . .

W 3. Like most women . . .

W 1. And artists. Especially the great ones. Yes. Those with real guts . . . The conquerors . . .

HE. You know what is our undoing, we're morons. Too modest.

W 2. Absolutely.

M 2. And in addition, you're not logical. You want to rely on what you feel, and nothing else . . . and when that leads you to . . . then you back down . . . oh, no, not that way . . . you're afraid, you haven't the right. Look at him: with less than nothing, simply by letting him go, he arrives at crime. And why not? He's right . . .

SHE. A real crime. That was luck. A crime. Something monstrous. Something provided for in every form of jurisprudence. But we . . . you see . . . izzum never ends with things like that . . .

HE. Izzum . . . if you follow it to its source . . . it takes us to . . .

SHE *(very softly)*. The inexpressible. Which has no name. Which has nowhere been provided for. Which nothing forbids.

HE. Something slippery . . . that runs through your fingers.

SHE. You catch it for a second. Romanticizzum. Capitalizzum. Syndicalizzum. Structuralizzum. It's that ending in zum. He holds it erect . . . it's like a scorpion's tail. It stings us . . . It ejects it's poison into us . . . to punish us . . . just for those words . . . for their ending . . .

HE. Surreptitiously he tries to destroy in us . . . oh, it's too insane, it's too mad! . . . a sort of vital point in us . . .

SHE. Quietly, slyly, no one the wiser.

HE. And through us, he gets at, sneers at . . . something . . .

SHE. He hates all that with his every fibre . . . they both do . . .

HE. A way of being . . . of thinking . . . *(Choking.)* Thought . . . They want to level . . . demean . . .

SHE. With complete impunity. Without our being able to make a move . . . without anybody ever daring . . . you wonder if you yourself aren't mad . . .

HE.   And nobody! Nobody to uphold us.

M 2 *(laughing)*.   Have you ever tried to speak to him about it?

HE.   Speak of that? To Dubuit?

M 2.   In your place, I would have taken the bull by the horns, if only to see: I would have said: see here, my friend, its *ism*. Izzum offends my ear.

SHE *(laughing)*.   Just to think of it, in fact, gives me a fit of nervous laughter. Wouldn't that give him the right to call the police for help? To have us hospitalized? . . .

HE.   Certainly. In a special type of hospital . . . *(Laughing.)* No, you surely don't think of doing that . . .

M 3.   They're right. In the present state of our legal system, they're beaten in advance. What they would need . . .

M 2.   I was thinking of that. They have such a strong sense . . . you have such a strong sense of legality, that you would need . . .

HE *(lower)*.   What we'd need would be for that, just that way of sneering, of sullying . . . just that slight accent . . . for that to be *forbidden by law*.

SHE.   Yes. Just that sly impulse to attack, to destroy . . . just that need to do harm . . . for that alone, with everybody's approval, to be able to seize them . . .hold them . . .

HE.   And force them to confess. . .

SHE.   Oh, what a relief that would be . . .

HE.   Yes, to drag that out of them . . . To expose it in broad daylight! Dry out . . . Burn it . . .

SHE.   Everything would be cleansed. Everything would be purified. They. We. We might even forgive . .'.

W 3.   Forgive? No, there I think you make a mistake. It would come out elsewhere. Your izzum would soon be replaced. Believe me, you'd see something else appear . . .

W 1.   That's true. With things like that you fill in here, they seep in there . . .

W 2.   You think so?

W 1.   I'm convinced of it. It's like a metastasis in the case of a person with cancer . . . Izzum . . . that's only a sign. A symptom.

SHE.   Yes. Izzum . . . izzum . . . like the little tell-tale pimple that gives you evidence of the pest . . .

W 3.   Like the single little lapse of good-breeding that, by itself alone, can reveal a lack of upbringing . . .

W 1.   Yes, yes. Which makes it possible immediately to classify, with no risk of being mistaken . . .

HE.   That's it, that's it, you're right. To classify. To set apart. In a closed category. In a cage. And we on the outside. A jail.

SHE.   And we . . . we, watching through the grating. The guilty man

is there, head shaven, wearing a uniform with a number on it.
And what did he do?

HE. He said izzum, stressing the zum. He said it to destroy, to
overthrow . . . And from now on, it will be punished — legally.
Izzum — just that. No other proofs are needed. Don't duck. Don't
try to get away. We've got you. We know you. People know. You
are the enemy. You dared . . . from below, as usual, believing you
were safe . . . Those are things you used to do, aren't they? When yo
thought you could do anything you wanted? But now . . . all that
has been divulged, it's known, classified, has a name. It's evil itself.
You are evil itself.

HE *laughing softly.*

SHE. Why are you laughing?

HE. You amuse me. You make me think of the frog in the fable. There
you are all puffed up . . . and it would be enough for them to be
there in front of you . . . You as torturer, as exterminator! . . . that's
a good one . . . When they're present . . . If anyone so much as took
the liberty with them . . . to make the slightest criticism . . . not even
for a little izzum . . . you would leap into the breach . . . a real moth
hen . . . not in my presence, I don't allow that . . . it's disgraceful . . .
they're so kind, so nice . . . *(Imitating her)*. . . They are our friends,
don't forget that . . . You remember when we were walking along
the water's edge and he leaned down . . . with what fervor . . . with
near piety . . . without picking it — to look . . . you remember . . .
for that alone . . .

SHE *(sad)*. Yes. I liked him.

M 2. Well, like him, then.

SHE. Yes, yes, I thank you for the advice . . . but that's just it, I've
already told you this . . . when I think I've succeeded, all at once,
there's a sort of odour, a whiff of something repugnant, that seeps
from them . . .

W 2. You see yourself, protruding ears . . . that's marvelous. That's
guaranteed to be effective. Ears — or toes — they're first class.
That's undeniable. That's evident. Nothing could eliminate them.
No pity. No emotion. No little spring flowers. And ears alone arouse
in those who have that good fortune, something sound, something
that's clear, pure. I assure you that when you've experienced that,
you yourself feel that you're made of a substance that is unalloyed.

W 1. That's true: you're like a diamond . . . and on the contrary,
people with protruding ears . . .

W 2. By that alone — without izzum, without anything, without their
knowing it themselves. No need to accuse them, no need to make the
confess . . .

M 4. Everything, absolutely everything that you might feel is justified,

All the izzums, all the accents . . .

SHE. Yes, I see perfectly. But the Dubuits haven't got protruding ears. Besides, you know, as far as we're concerned, protruding ears make no difference to us.

HE. No, none really. They leave me cold.

W 2. You'll notice, however, that that's not the only thing. I took protruding ears because I had somebody in mind . . . But an exaggeratedly long upper lip, for instance . . . for certain people . . .

W 1. Yes. For me. I have a horror of that.

W 3. Or a protruding lower jaw . . . like this . . . you see what I mean . . . I must say that I . . . ugh . . . You don't? Really? Nothing like that?

SHE. No. Frankly . . . practically nothing. I can't say that I adore that . . . but after all . . . how about you?

HE. I don't either, obviously. But it's amorphous, it's passive . . . it has no venom . . . not to be compared . . .

M 3. With your izzum. I assure you, there's a screw loose about that . . .

M 2. I told you so. You made fun of me when I tried to relieve them.

W 1. Oh, yes, with the isthmus of Panama!

SHE. No, no, not that!

M 2. Did you hear her? What véhemence! What resistance! Believe me, the source is there. As for me . . . the more I observe them, the more I'm convinced of it. No possible doubt: the seat of the malady is there.

Silence.

SHE. Listen: romanticizzum. Capitalizzum. Syndicalizzum . . . zum . . . zum . . . with a smack . . . he smacks his lips . . .

HE. He relishes it . . . yumyum, that's good. Izzum.

SHE. It passes smoothly . . . like the sharp edge of a blade of grass.

HE. Izumm. Izzum . . .

SHE. It cuts you . . . it sinks in . . .

HE. And through that . . . but how does it happen that you don't feel it? . . .

SHE. Try, I beg of you, say it like this, stressing . . . izzum . . . izzum . . . do you feel it?

W 3. Yes, perhaps, if I try very hard . . .

M 2. Very hard, indeed. Personally, I must admit that for me . . . syndicalizzum, structuralizzum. However often I repeat it . . . izzum. Izzum . . . perhaps . . . yes, if you like . . . there is, in fact . . .

M 3. Yes. I see . . .

SHE. Oh! It's not possible! You do see? . . .

M 3. Ye . . . e . . . es . . . Although to tell the truth . . .

SHE. To tell the truth?

M 3 *(hesitating)*. No . . . It's nothing . . . It's really . . . No . . . it's really what you might call nothing.

The Lie

Translated by Maria Jolas

Le mensonge (The Lie) was first performed 14 January 1967 at the Théâtre de France, to celebrate the inauguration of the Petit Odéon, with the following cast:

YVONNE	Catherine Rethi
LUCIE	Annie Bertin
SIMONE	Nelly Benedetti
JULIETTE	Marie-Christine Barrault
JEANNE	Anne Carrère
JACQUES	Dominique Paturel
ROBERT	Jean-Pierre Granval
PIERRE	Gabriel Cattand
VINCENT	Amidou

Directed by Jean-Louis Barrault

YVONNE.   I felt like crawling into a hole.

LUCIE.   So did I. I didn't know which way to turn.

SIMONE.   Oh, it was ghastly.

JACQUES.   I couldn't believe my ears. Styvers. I thought I must be
dreaming. To mention that name . . . in front of Madeleine . . .

ROBERT.   In front of Madeleine? He mentioned Styvers? That's not
possible . . .

SIMONE.   So you're not able to control yourself?

LUCIE.   I didn't dare look at her.

YVONNE.   She was painful to see. She literally shrivelled up . . .
became absolutely grey . . .

ROBERT.   I should say, after all, she hides that as though it were
something to ashamed of.

JACQUES.   Personally, I avoid the subject, even from afar . . . I take
my precautions . . . But you . . . what are you made of, anyway?
How do you have the nerve? I'd rather die . . .

PIERRE.   I couldn't stand it any longer . . . really, she goes too
far. There's a limit, after all . . . What does she take us for?
Morons? You should have heard her. *(He imitates a woman's
voice)* 'Did you see that they've raised the fares? We'll have to walk.
Nobody will be able to afford the tube . . . It's poor devils like us
who always bear the brunt . . . 'And there they were listening . . .
You should have seen them . . . Nodding approval . . . You could
hear them sighing.. . .

YVONNE.   Oh, sighing . . . you're overdoing it . . .

PIERRE.   Not at all. You were on the point of pitying her. Everybody
lets her get away with it, no one dares to make a move . . . Finally
it got the better of me, I exploded . . .

LUCIE.   That's true. It came out like a canon ball. Styvers! You
shouted it . . .

PIERRE.   No, I didn't shout, it seems to me that it was more like a
whistle. It had been boiling up for some time. *(He imitates himself)*
'Why, I thought you were Styver's granddaughter . . . his only heir.
Gossip has it . . . It is he, isn't it, who is the famous steel-baron?
Did you see what happened then?

SIMONE.   No, I didn't want to see, it was too awful.

JACQUES.   I don't understand by what right . . . that's her affair,
after all. She asks nothing of anybody . . .

ROBERT.   Why, of course. Personally, she amuses me. In reality there
are lots like her. It's unbelievable how many people are ashamed

73

of having money. Have you noticed, everybody would
like to have a working-class father. I think that's rather a healthy
sign . . .

SIMONE. Yes, it's quite the thing just now, the 'worker' pose . . .
It is a pose . . . Particularly among intellectuals . . . They even lay
it on . . . in their way of speaking . . . their clothes . . .

VINCENT. Perhaps they do . . . in such things . . . you're right . . .
but with Madeleine that's not the case, with her it's not a pose . . .
I'm inclined to think it's a matter of prudence: she must be
stingy . . . I'll admit, however, that she overdoes it, she irritates
me . . . but from that to Pierre's daring to . . .

YVONNE. But Pierre is so uncompromising, so intolerant . . . Do
you know, Pierre dear, who you remind me of? That character
in I forget which novel, about whom someone said: he never lets
anyone tell a fib . . .

LUCIE. That's true. Pierre, you're awful . . . nobody can set himself
up like that, as the righter of all wrongs, the supreme judge . . .
That doesn't suit you, I assure you.

PIERRE. But I told you that it just spurted out in spite of myself
. . . It was like a sort of pressure . . . Nothing . . . neither the wheel,
nor the stake . . .

JULIETTE *(with naive seriousness)*. It's truth that presses like that.
In Pierre's defence it must be said that when truth starts pressing, it .

JEANNE. Yes indeed! it's hard to hold back . . . You're right. It requir
such *lebensraum,* you have no idea . . . It has a force of expansion . .

JACQUES. I must admit that when Madeleine gets started, I too,
at times, begin to feel itchy . . .

JULIETTE. Yes, I think she's getting worse and worse . . .

SIMONE. That's true. It seems to me that she used to be more
retiring, that she did it more unobtrusively . . . But now, these
perpetual lamentations . . .

JEANNE. I must say that if I were her, I don't know, but I shouldn't
dare . . . I'd be so frightened . . . I never could, even for the
slightest thing . . . To begin with my father, ever since we were
little . . . In our family they were terribly strict about that . . .
And then, it would never have occurred to me . . .

VINCENT. All the same, to be that transparent . . . must be rather
painful . . .

JEANNE. Not at all, I have a horror of lying. Even about little things,
I never could do it . . .

JACQUES. Why do you smile, Pierre?

PIERRE. Did I smile?

JACQUES. Yes, with a look of . . . One always wonders with you . . .
you give me such an impression of being a lie-detector . . .

PIERRE. Why? Who lied?

JACQUES.   Nobody. But since Jeanne said she *never* lied . . . it
was the word *never* . . . So I thought . . . since that's so unusual
. . . It seemed to me that you immediately . . . that is . . . I
had the impression it was beginning again . . . You smiled . . .

ROBERT.   Now listen, enough of that, It's contagious, and now
you've caught it . . .

JULIETTE.   Truth is pressing in him too. And when truth starts
pressing, I told you . . .

JEANNE.   How kind, indeed . . .

JACQUES.   No Jeanne, don't believe it, it's not you . . . But since
it seemed to me . . . since the slightest overstatement . . .

PIERRE.   No no, don't listen to him, there's no connection . . . In
Madeleine's case, it's not a matter of overstatement, but of
enormities, facts . . . It's something that's there, in us, and then
when we want to repress it, it starts pressing . . . it has to come
out . . . it's like trying to repress . . . oh, I don't know . . .

LUCIE.   Now, listen! Where would it lead to if each one of us was like
that, continually . . . But people make an effort, they control
themselves . . .

SIMONE.   It's a simple matter of practice, self-control . . .

ROBERT.   As for that, I must say that, personally, and I don't mean
to boast, but, personally, truth, well, it can keep on pressing . . .
with me, I control it, I assure you . . . it's tamed . . . You have to,
otherwise, how could you live?

SIMONE.   But you know that's marvellous, You know that's a sign
of splendid health. I read in a book on psychiatry that a person who
can't keep a secret . . .

YVONNE.   There we are. That was just the thing to say, What does
truth do to you Pierre, when its a question of keeping a secret?
Does it press or not press?

PIERRE.   Of course, it continues to press. sometimes even, it hurts.
You have the feeling that you're going to burst . . . But there are cases
of course . . . you're obliged to resist . . . You've given your word . . .
common decency . . . You know what I mean . . .

YVONNE.   Ah! you see . . .

PIERRE.   What do I see? That I should restrain myself with
Madeleine? Out of common decency? That's a bit too much . . .
I ask you, who is lacking in common decency, she or I?

JULIETTE.   It's true, she's pulling our leg.

VINCENT.   I must say, I too . . . when she starts snivelling about
how poor she is . . . Some day I'm going to do like Pierre, I'm going
to explode . . .

PIERRE.   You see. He says it too. It's terrible when it starts to press . . .
You could kill your own grandmother . . .

JEANNE. You could even kill yourself. There've been such cases.

PIERRE. Look at Socrates . . .

JACQUES. Now please, you're not going to compare yourself to Socrates.

SIMONE. We're the ones who are dying: you're torturing us so that little tuppenny truth of yours can win out.

YVONNE. 'Take care of the pennies . . .' was never more appropriate. But who cares, really, if Madeleine's grandfather . . .

LUCIE. Everybody does that more or less. Telling fibs . . . People have to improve their image, after all . . . They do the best they can.

YVONNE. Personally, I think they're more to be pitied than anything else.

ROBERT. I think they're amusing. I must admit that I even like it. I love to watch them.

JULIETTE. You like it? When people lie to you? I call that vicious . . .

ROBERT. Perhaps it is . . . But as I told you: for me, truth, on leash. Tamed. It can try to come out as much as it wants: there's not a chance. I don't even have to make an effort. For instance, when Pierre exploded, on the contrary, I would have looked straight at Madeleine . . .

VINCENT. Oh, you disgust me . . .

JEANNE. Hypocrite.

ROBERT. After all, what do you expect? It's when you explode that you expose yourself. Look at Pierre. Everybody jumped on him. 'Wretch. Scoundrel. How low-minded can you be? How savage?' They called him a murderer. Meanwhile the other person is innocent, the one people defend. 'Common decency . . . They have the right after all . . . Let them lie, just a little . . . ' Personally, I let them do it. As much as they want. No brakes, ever. And I don't suffer, I assure you. Not the slightest discomfiture. That would be all that was needed.

JULIETTE. But how? How do you do it?

ROBERT. I really don't know . . . It's rather hard to explain. It's a matter of instinct . . . We act in a certain way, without even thinking . . .

JULIETTE (avidly). Yes, I understand, without thinking . . . With certain people, it just happens. It's always like that with privileged people, they never give a thought, they have only to let matters take their course, and presto, without any effort, they do the right thing . . .

JEANNE. Yes, but we're not that fortunate, we suffer, you could just show us . . .

ROBERT.   But how do you mean?

JULIETTE.   Yes show us. I feel sure we could learn. I feel sure that I could succeed in being like you, even to being delighted with it . . . There's a trick you have to learn, I feel it . . .

JACQUES.   They're right. Give us a demonstration.

SIMONE.   It must be a matter of practice.

JULIETTE.   Like limbering-up exercises . . . I think I've guessed it; we're too stiff.

JEANNE.   Gymnastics, in other words . . .

ROBERT.   Yes, if you want, it's a bit like that . . . or perhaps boxing, rather, when you come to think of it . . .

JEANNE.   Quick, I want to have a lesson.

ROBERT.   Very well, if you want . . .

YVONNE.   Oh! that will be fun. It will be like a psycho-drama . . .

ROBERT.   Well let's start . . . But somebody will have to be 'it' . . . the liar.

VINCENT.   I'll be glad to.

PIERRE.   Fine. You seem to me to be just the right one.

VINCENT.   You're not funny. I assure you.

PIERRE.   No, that's true. Forgive me, but whose role will it be? Which liar? There are so many, of all kinds . . .

ROBERT.   Oh! it doesn't matter. But let's take someone who knows how, someone with whom you have had a hard time restraining yourself, someone who can make the most hardened listener suffer, Edgar, why not, when he starts telling about his feats of resistance . . . Then, you'll admit, you need real force . . .

JACQUES.   Very well. Edgar. That's fine. Even I, when he gets going . . .

ROBERT.   So it's all set for Edgar. You play Edgar. Go ahead. Begin. Unassumingly . . .

JULIETTE.   And very openly . . . No, really, just the thought of it . . . makes me sick . . .

SIMONE.   That's right . . . Edgar is fine. So go ahead.

VINCENT.   Now then *(clearing his throat)*. Wait. I think I've got it. *(Change of voice)*.   'You know I dislike courage. I have a horror of it.'

YVONNE.   Very good. That's how he usually starts.

VINCENT.   The fact is that I am very easily frightened, you know I'm a real coward.

SIMONE.   That's it exactly. That's perfect. You would make a splendid actor.

VINCENT.   Yes, I'm very easily frightened . . . Really . . .

ROBERT.   Well . . . Nobody makes a move? It seems to me that if we were in earnest, at that moment somebody . . . You Lucie, for instance . . .

77

LUCIE. It's because I don't quite see myself. It's not as though it were in earnest.

ROBERT. In earnest, my dear, you would not have let him continue . . . 'You a coward! You. Edgar, easily frightened! You who showed . . . ' It's pitiful to witness . . .

PIERRE. That's true, Lucie, you know you can't help it.

LUCIE. You're right. I can't help it . . . I always have to anticipate his moves . . . as though he were pulling me . . .

VINCENT. Poor Lucie . . . she's so docile . . .

PIERRE. So pliable.

LUCIE. That's right, make fun of me, it's so easy . . . It's because I feel pity for people. The rest of you are capable of not giving a thing when a man — or not even a man: when a hungry animal looks at you, and waits? . . . You give him something . . . you prefer to deprive yourself . . .

YVONNE. Yes, I understand you . . . It's true, he makes me feel sorry for him . . . If I were he I'd be afraid . . . he must tremble . . .

VINCENT. He tremble! Now listen, people like that are dumb brutes. They're aware of nothing . . . they're convinced that you believe them . . . Or if they aren't convinced all they care about is for you to be taken in. That's enough for them. That's their way of making you give in . . .

PIERRE. And you always give in . . . Lucie's not the only one. You're all so sensitive . . . As soon as he starts, you become wide-eyed . . . you look absolutely dumbfounded: 'You. Edgar, how can you say that . . . '

JULIETTE. Not I, I don't. At the very start, I hold my own, I don't flinch, I say nothing . . .

JACQUES. But what difference does it make, if you say nothing or not? Silence gives consent, it's all the same.

JEANNE. Oh! listen, we're getting bogged down . . . I thought Robert was supposed to teach us . . . Robert, darling, help, get us out of this . . .

ROBERT. How do you expect me to do it? I'm not allowed to speak . . .

JULIETTE. I must admit that I'm all at sea, I think we should start all over again . . .

JEANNE. She's right, we've lost the thread . . . Go ahead, Vincent, start again . . .

VINCENT. You know. I'm easily frightened . . . which is why, during the occupation, when I had to . . .

ROBERT. Now Lucie, this time you continue . . .

LUCIE. But perhaps it's better for me to say nothing . . .

ROBERT. No I prefer for you to speak. It makes the demonstration

78

easier . . . You'll see . . .

LUCIE You, Edgar, you easily frightened!

ROBERT. Good. How do you feel when you say that? Or rather, where are you?

LUCIE. Where am I?

ROBERT. Yes, with regard to Edgar, how far away? In what position?

LUCIE. Ah, yes, I see . . . Wait a second . . . let me think . . . because I'm not accustomed . . . things like that . . . I don't know . . .

ROBERT. Make an effort. Break up the action. What happens when you say that? What are you doing?

LUCIE. Well, it seems to me that I'm trying to make a rapprochement . . . I want to cling to him, quite close . . . as close as possible . . . so that he doesn't realise I can see him . . . that would frighten me . . . I dont know why . . .

ROBERT. Well, as it happens, you must keep away. At a distance. Very far. Distance is essential. Watch him, the way we watch an ant, a fly, or, if you prefer, a spider.

LUCIE. Oh, no! I can't do that . . .

ROBERT. If you can't even do that at the beginning, then really . . .

LUCIE. Very well, I'll try. Now then Vincent, let's begin again.

VINCENT. 'I've always been easily frightened. When I was a child, at school . . . '

LUCIE. You, Edgar, you easily frightened . . .

ROBERT. Now then, this time where were you?

LUCIE. It can't be helped, I can't do it. I was quite near, nearer than before. I was clinging to him to help him hold it back . . . the truth . . . to hide it, to let it disappear . . . I was so afraid that he would think I saw it . . . I can't bear it . . . it would make me feel so embarrassed.

ROBERT. But that's just it, I tell you not to take part. Keep away. At an enormous distance. Observe his movements from afar . . . As though you were teasing an insect with a twig . . . And you were waiting to see. Enjoy yourself a bit. All together now, let's get on with it. You'll feel solid on the ground. Try it. At a distance. Don't lean forwards. Stand straight. Teasing him with a long stem. Go ahead . . .

CHORUS. You Edgar, you easily frightened. . .

ROBERT. Now then. You're baiting him. You're leading him on. Greek meets Greek. He falls into the trap. That's not funny?

SIMONE. Not at all. I can't do it. Such cynicism as that . . .

JACQUES. I don't want to become like him. That would be even more painful. I don't feel like imitating him.

LUCIE. Oh! that makes my flesh creep . . .

JACQUES. You know, I'm no entomologist and Edgar is not an ant.

JULIETTE. And what about truth? Because it presses you, you forget that . . . That's what hurts . . . when you hold it back it swells, it must come out . . . I'm like Pierre, I feel like shouting. Oh no, don't start talking to us about your exploits . . . Nobody's fooled. Everybody knows . . . '

ROBERT. Really you are all impossible. Explode, then, like Pierre. Or else suffer.

JEANNE. But it's funny, Robert, that you shouldn't feel such things as that. You're not made like other people, believe me.

JULIETTE. There are people . . . in whom it presses so hard . . . that they're capable . . .

JACQUES. Yes, as someone said a while ago, there are people . . . for it to prevail . . . I'm not even speaking of saints and heroes. It's far more extraordinary than that. Informers, for instance. I knew a baker during the occupation . . . It was not out of hatred. Not out of conviction. No, truth was simply pressing in him. He couldn't stand it: all the false names, the false papers . . . and everybody taken in. It had to come out . . . I'm sure that, in the same way, he might have saved . . .

VINCENT. No. There you overdo it. You're not going to make a little saint out of that spy of yours . . .

JACQUES. But I'm not joking.

SIMONE. You may be right. I remember, during the war . . . There were some Canadian parachutists . . . my husband had met them in the woods. They were running away and my husband ran towards them, his arms outstretched . . . Finally he succeeded in bringing them to our house.

PIERRE. So it's you now who are playing the role, I don't understand anything any more . . .

SIMONE. What role? I'm not playing! That really happened. We were living in the Seine et Oise . . .

PIERRE. You were living in the Seine et Oise during the occupation?

ROBERT. There we are, the lie detector has started up again.

LUCIE. Stop, I beg of you. Let Simone tell us . . . I love her stories. . .

PIERRE. Really, Lucie dear, you're hopeless . . .

YVONNE. Oh, you, over there, be silent. It gets to be a bore. You never believe anybody.

PIERRE. She was not in the Seine et Oise, since she was in Switzerland all during the war . . . But she's joking, she wants to go on playing. She'll say it. Do say it, Simone. Say you're playing.

80

SIMONE. I'm not playing, I tell you. It's *true*.

PIERRE. But you told me yourself . . .

SIMONE. I? I didn't tell you anything at all, you're dreaming . . . You must confuse . . .

PIERRE. Oh, very well. I won't say anything more . . . I'll stop talking . . .

YVONNE. Then really stop talking. You're insufferable. Go ahead. Simone tell us . . .

SIMONE. Well, as I was saying, when my husband saw these parachutists he started to run after them and they thought he was trying to take them prisoner, however much he shouted and waved his arms . . . Finally they understood. He brought them back to the house . . . They were in such a state . . .

PIERRE *(groaning)*. Oh . . .

JACQUES. What's the matter?

PIERRE. Oh, I can't stand it any longer . . . So you weren't in Geneva during the war?

SIMONE. So I'm lying?

PIERRE. Oh, no! No! I didn't say that. But you're playing. You're playing a joke on us.

SIMONE. I tell you no, and that's that . . . you bore me stiff . . .

YVONNE. Leave her alone, will you?

PIERRE. No, leave us alone a moment . . . Simone, I beg of you, listen to me, I may be wrong, but it seems to me . . . I remember that you said . . .

SIMONE. That I said what?

PIERRE. You said that you were in Geneva . . .

SIMONE But my dear Pierre, I've already said that you were dreaming . . . You confuse everything . . .

PIERRE. How can you? You know perfectly . . .

SIMONE. I know nothing at all. Except that your cheek . . .

PIERRE *(groaning)*. Oh . . . I can't bear it . . . she's trying to provoke me . . . Simone. listen to me, listen calmly, it would be so simple, after all . . .

VINCENT. Stop him, he's intolerable.

JACQUES. It's true. So there. Calm yourselves. What are you driving at anyway? You see perfectly well that you'll never get anywhere. Don't you think we'd better change?

PIERRE. Change? The truth? Why, I can't. It's impossible.

JACQUES. Yes, you can, you can, you can do it perfectly well, all that's needed is a little good will.

SIMONE. You too, now are beginning to insult me . . .

JACQUES. Not at all, Simone dear, don't be angry. I believe you. But since he's suffering . . . without cause . . . we must help . . . be kind.

81

SIMONE. I wish you joy . . .

PIERRE. No, don't be beastly, all I want is to believe you . . .
I'd be so glad . . .

JACQUES. Well then believe her, hang it! And let's drop the
subject.

PIERRE. But how can I? It's there inside me . . .

JACQUES. What? What is it that's there?

PIERRE. The facts. The truth. It's there.

JACQUES. First, begin by not calling that the truth. Change
it's name. It's a name that as soon as its spoken, impresses
people. They hang on to it as if their very life depended on
it . . . They believe they're obliged . . . That should be changed
. . . call it lying . . .

PIERRE. That's not so easy . . .

JACQUES. Oh, now listen, if you refuse to be a bit more
supple . . . If each one of us is going to cling to his own
little personal dignity . . . Then, what do you expect me to
tell you . . .

PIERRE. No, go ahead, please tell me . . .

JACQUES. But I did tell you: you've got to change. It's better
to change oneself than to change the world, that's the part of
wisdom . . .

PIERRE. Teach me, I'll never succeed.

ROBERT. What's going on? Are we putting on another
demonstration?

SIMONE. No, no. This is reality. I'm not playing. But poor Pierre
here has got hold of a fact that has become embedded inside
him: it seems that I was in Geneva all during the war. So he's
suffering, it hurts him. It should be taken out. It appears to be a
rather painful operation. . .

JACQUES. No, you'll see, it'll be nothing at all. Above all, Pierre,
relax . . . There . . . now don't get tense . . . To begin with, are you
sure of it? Try to remember. Did she say that?

PIERRE. Yes, she said it.

JACQUES. Wait, I'm going to help you. Look at her well. It's not
possible that she would lie. Splendid! That's the way to do it,
you'll see, it'll all come out. Observe how frank she looks, the
fine directness of her gaze.

JEANNE. Yes, Simone, you look as though butter wouldn't melt in
your mouth.

LUCIE. That's true, would she look like that?

PIERRE. That doesn't mean a thing, that's happened before . . . And
even in cases . . . I remember, one time, before a Grand Jury . . .

JULIETTE. Oh, no, listen, that's ridiculous. Now you're making a
criminal out of her.

82

SIMONE. I'm beginning to feel quite flattered.

PIERRE. No, after all . . . I just meant to say . . .

JACQUES. Listen, let's not be led astray. Here we're amongst honest citizens.

Several voices.

Well, of course.

That's even our misfortune.

JULIETTE. I must admit frankly. I too, I had been told that Simone . . . I was practically certain of it . . . Well, now I'm beginning to have my doubts . . . things are getting blurred. I no longer feel that pressure . . . as though you were being torn in two . . .

JACQUES. You see, she gives you an example.

PIERRE. But I want nothing better than to believe, Simone, if you'd only help me a bit . . . That story about the parachutists . . . now it all comes back to me . . . you had told it before . . . perhaps already during the occupation . . . tell me you did, Simone, tell me . . .

SIMONE. Of course not, I couldn't have told that under the occupation. We were hiding at that time.

PIERRE. Yes, yes that's right, at that time, you could not have told it. But after the liberation, probably . . .

SIMONE. Yes, afterwards, I did tell it. One evening, for instance at the Ducreux's . . . you were there . . .

PIERRE. Oh . ... at the Ducreux's . . . But it seems to me that on that same evening, you told me . . .

Voices

Oh, oh! watch out . . .

There he goes again . . .

ROBERT. No. I was there. She did tell it. That's all she said.

PIERRE. Oh! thank you. Yes, I believe you. At times I have memory blocks, so much has happened.

JACQUES. Now you see. I don't want to brag, but my advice would be to . . . That succeeds even in the more serious cases . . .

ROBERT. What cases?

JACQUES. Well, for instance, when you were robbed. An object disappears. And yet that is what you might call a certainty: it's no longer there, its gone, vanished into thin air . . . It was there and . . . suddenly . . . there's nothing . . .

YVONNE. I should say so, in such cases, how you do suffer! You can't believe your eyes.

JEANNE *(avidly)*. That's it, that's it. How right you are! You can't believe your eyes.

JACQUES. Exactly. You *must* not believe them.

PIERRE. But how?

JACQUES. Forget the object. Concentrate on the human being: the person you suspect, the thief . . . Observe him: his frank manner. Open. Kind. And keep saying to yourself: 'It's not possible. . . ' The way people do . . . with that dumbfounded look they have, when someone says: 'He's the one. The object that was there has disappeared and only he could . . . ' They thrust this fact aside and look at the man: 'It's not possible . . . the object will be found' . . . They even go further, I've seen some of them: the object had never existed. It has been a hallucination. A mirage. There had been no object. Out of sight, out of mind. A sensory illusion, a phantasmagoria.

YVONNE. Yes, I do that too. Otherwise . . . oh, I'm frightened. . .

JEANNE. The soul's abyss is slowly opening. Noxious vapours are rising . . we are asphyxiating . . .

VINCENT. There are others . . . They start to beg . . . 'You took it: confess. I don't care about the object, I'll give it to you, but confess . . . '

PIERRE. Confess, Simone, I beg of you . . .

SIMONE. What's the matter? Ah! So you're off: you're starting all over again?

PIERRE. Yes, I'm off again. There it is, all of a sudden . . . something, quite clear, written for all to read, I can't help it, I see it. There it is The Epervier, the Hotel de l'Epervier. In Geneva. You yourself said it to me . . . It doesn't help, to make things uncertain, to rub them out . . . There it is. Say it . . .

YVONNE. That'll do Pierre.

JEANNE. If I were Simone.

VINCENT. You're going too far . . .

PIERRE. That doesn't make you laugh, Simone, to see them? It doe doesn't it? they amuse you . . . admit it, they're really touching . . so ingenuous . . . or frightened . . . But I myself see you. Your bac seeing eye . . .

LUCIE. Dear Lord . . .

JULIETTE. What's the matter? What's all the shouting about?

YVONNE. It's Lucie. She's so sensitive, poor darling . . . After all, I understand her . . . You'd think you were in a mad-house . . . There now . . . my dear, don't be afraid, it's nothing, don't listen . . . stop your ears . . .

LUCIE. Oh, restrain him, make him control himself, you can't . . . I can't stand . . .

JACQUES. Yes, Pierre, keep quiet, take it back. Nobody believes you. It's not true.

PIERRE. No, you won't succeed in doing it. When you say that,

it becomes engraved even more deeply, it sinks in, burns . . .
Simone, I beg of you, Simone dear, it's there in you too . . .
don't deny it, I know you're repressing it . . . it's there
you know that very well: l'Hôtel de l'Epervier, on the edge of
the lake . . . and those four years in Geneva. Your evening with
the Ruffier's . . . in their chalet . . . your mountain excursions
. . . It hurts you too, poor dear . . . it's hard to repress that . . .
when it would be so easy . . . just one single word . . .

JULIETTE. I feel that in me too . . . A while ago it had disappeared,
and then now . . . in spite of myself, it's coming back.

JEANNE. That's the truth . . . it's rising, it's attracted . . . It's
irresistible . . . you can't help it . . . Listen, Simone . . .

SIMONE. No. You're lying. The entire lot of you. It's shameful.

LUCIE. Oh! I'm frightened.

YVONNE. Lucie darling, come over here, to one side, let's both
stay here, let's think about something else . . . I was just going
to ask you how is Claude?

LUCIE (in a lifeless tone). He's well, thank you, very well.

YVONNE. I heard that he had undergone . . .

LUCIE. Yes, yes, but please, go and see, just come and tell
me what's happening? What are they doing to her?

YVONNE. To Simone?

LUCIE. Yes . . . It seemed to me that he mentioned poison, a
phial to be opened.

YVONNE. He's very funny. He compares her to poisoners . . .
when they pour a few drops, then observe their victims.

LUCIE. I can't stand it any longer. I prefer to go and see.

JEANNE. Simone, don't resist.

JULIETTE. Tell us.

VINCENT. Do tell us . . . Just one word . . .

LUCIE. Well, it was as I feared, they're aroused . . . Their greed,
their avidity are roused, they're going to snatch it from her,
they're after her, they're pressing her, their iron rods are probing,
she's withdrawn into her hole . . . a little hunted animal . . . her
frightened eyes observing them, she's all warm and quivering . . . and
I like her . . .

YVONNE. But you're dreaming. She's looking at them with an icy gaze.

ROBERT. I think it's what's called 'if looks could kill.' Her look is
killing them.

JULIETTE. Simone, don't say no . . . Tell it . . . Tell us . . . now we must
know . . .

JEANNE. It's become a thing of great price . . . in your possession . . .
Hidden there, buried in you . . . like a treasure.

SIMONE. The Hôtel de l'Epervier?

JULIETTE. No, don't make fools of us, that's not funny.

PIERRE. Let us in. Let us see. We must. Share with us. That would be so nice. That would be such happiness . . . A relief to everybody.

JEANNE. No more heartrending scenes . . . for you, either . . . We'd be so calm. Everything would be as before.

JULIETTE. Wait, it's coming. She's about to give in. Look at her, her lips are moving. In a second, the words . . .

LUCIE. Simone, I beg of you, don't give in. They're trying to destroy you, to exhaust you. They're going to grab you, put your neck into a noose, shave your head.

PIERRE. No, Simone that's not true . . . We're like you . . . all alike . . . nobody wants to demean you . . .

JACQUES. Just the thought of it makes us shrink . . . Like a while ago with Madeleine . . .

PIERRE. No, believe us, it will be with the most honourable intentions . . . Say it, that will be so nice . . . say it, say of course I was in Geneva. I was playing . . .

SIMONE *laughs*

LUCIE. Oh! That laugh . . .

SIMONE *(laughing)*. Oh, all right, of course, I was playing . . . There. Are you satisfied?

Sound of happy laughter, kissing, clucking.

JULIETTE. Simone, you're a darling.

VINCENT. You're an angel.

JEANNE. Simone, I adore you.

JACQUES. I never had a moment's doubt. I knew it. I saw that sly little look of yours . . .

ROBERT. I must say you played a good trick on us . . .

JULIETTE. For a moment, I must confess that I was frightened . . .

JEANNE. Lucie was as pale as a sheet.

ROBERT. Yes, I noticed . . . Yvonne took her part. So Pierre, you are satisfied. Now we can have peace.

PIERRE. Yes. *(Hesitant)*. Yes . . .

ROBERT. But what's the matter now? You're not going to start again?

JACQUES. This time it's finished, do you hear?

PIERRE. Yes, of course . . . I ask nothing better . . . It's not my fault if . . .

VINCENT. If what? Simone said she was playing. That's all she was asked to say. That's not good enough for you?

PIERRE *(imitating SIMONE)*. Oh, all right, of course, I was playing .

ROBERT. What did you say?

PIERRE *(dreamily)*. I repeated what Simone said, with the same

laugh in the same tone . . . I tried to reproduce . . . the same movements . . . Further . . . still further . . . much further still than a
while ago . . . in a spot from where nobody can dislodge her . . .
And she throwing that at us as a feint, to keep us at arm's length . . .
Here, take this: I was playing. There. Are you satisfied?
They were funny, weren't they, Simone, when they grabbed at it . . .
how they chortled . . . how they groaned with pleasure . . .

JACQUES. Pierre, stop that, do you hear? Now, that's enough.

YVONNE. A cold shower, a straight-jacket . . .

JEANNE. It's shameful, I said so at the very first.

PIERRE. At the very first? You yourself didn't say? . . .
Who mentioned miasmas? The soul's abyss? What language,
in any case . . . what over-emphasis . . . Who asked us to stage
a psycho-drama? You or I?

JEANNE. You dragged us into it. They're contagious, all these mad
goings-on. . .

VINCENT. They're a matter of nerves . . . Like people scratching
themselves.

PIERRE. And all the sententious phrases about truth pressing?
Yet, that was so touching . . . Well, it's still pressing, I can't help
it. And it's pressing in her too: Oh, all right, I was playing . . . You saw
it just as I did . . . It fairly hit you in the eye, or rather in the eardrums.

JACQUES. Nothing. Nothing hit anything at all.

ROBERT. But he likes that. He battens on it.

YVONNE. I know of nothing pettier, more degrading. It's really
terrible to see evil everywhere.

PIERRE. I hadn't thought of it . . . It was quite unexpected, that
backward leap, at the last moment . . . By leaving that planted
in me: that little laugh . . . like a dart . . . Bravo Simone, that was
splendid, that was splendid, quite a feat . . . You may be pleased.

SIMONE. Delighted . . . And I shall be even more delighted when
they come to lock you in a cell. I assure you, that's where you
belong.

PIERRE *(avidly)*. Indeed, you think so? Really? In a cell?
You said that so well. With conviction. Good. Very good. It's
true isn't it? Where would we end up if, for every shade of . . .
hardly a shade . . . just a slightly derisive intonation . . . isn't that
so? Only slightly ironical. That you can't deny, you all heard it,
just as I did.

JACQUES. Of course, we heard a note of derision.

PIERRE. Ah! yes, you did? yes . . .

JACQUES. And quite naturally so: we had all been so easily taken
in.

PIERRE. Oh, thank you.

ROBERT. Don't mention it. If that can calm you, I can tell you
that almost anybody in Simone's place would have been in a
position to make a little fun of us: we had so dramatized things.

PIERRE. Yes, Simone, that's true isn't it?

SIMONE. Yes, it's true. But we've had enough now, it's no longer
funny . . .

YVONNE. Yes, that's enough. Suppose we think about something
else, Pierre, do you mind?

PIERRE. Do I mind? Why, that's what I want most. It's only . . . as
though something were there . . . planted . . . hardly perceptible
. . . and scratching . . . like a tiny cactus barb . . . it's as though I
had touched nettles . . . it barely smarts . . . ah, all right, of course,
I was playing . . . and that laugh . . . that little laugh . . . But
Simone, I'm mad, I'm quite mad. I love your indignant look,
your disgusted manner. If you knew how I love them, Simone.
Look at me. Again.

SIMONE. You don't have to beg me. I'm disgusted. Sincerely so, too.

PIERRE. Disgusted. Sincerely. Yes. Thank you. Disgusted? . . . The
way you said that . . . Like a while ago . . . when I tried to make
you admit . . . when you protested so much. 'That's disgraceful. I'm
not playing.' You said that so well. Exactly the same way.

SIMONE. This time, all of you, don't count on me.

YVONNE. I also think the joke has lasted long enough. We were
patient. Very patient.

PIERRE. She's avenged herself. Cleverly, too. I didn't leave her a leg
to stand on . . .

ROBERT. Good-bye, everybody. All good things must come to an end

PIERRE. And then she gave me what I was begging for . . . with a wor
in the apple.

VINCENT. Robert, let's leave together. I must speak to you.

PIERRE. With that little nettle . . . planted here. Oh, all right, of cour
(He laughs) . . . I was playing.

ROBERT. Simone, my dear, if I were you, I'd be flattered: that's wha
called driving a man crazy.

SIMONE. I could do without it.

PIERRE *(hesitant and sly).* Oh, all right, of course, I was playing . . . *(
a different, natural, frank tone)*Oh, all right, of course. I was playing
No. There, there's nothing, no derision.

JULIETTE. No derision? Why, how nice. You see, things are going
better. Come on, we'll take you home. You should rest, my dear,
you need it.

PIERRE. Yes, very well, I shall . . . *(A frank tone).*Oh, all right . . .
of course, I was playing. *(He laughs softly)* . . . Oh, all right, of cour
. . . *(Hypocritically)* I was playing . . .

Silence

Translated by Maria Jolas

Le silence (Silence) was first performed 14 January 1967 at the Théâtre de France to celebrate the inauguration of the Petit Odéon, with the following cast:

WOMAN 1	Madeleine Renaud
WOMAN 2	Paule Annen
WOMAN 3	Nelly Benedetti
WOMAN 4 (Marthe)	Marie-Christine Barrault
MAN 1	Dominique Paturel
MAN 2	Amidou
JEAN-PIERRE	Jean-Pierre Granval

Directed by Jean-Louis Barrault

W 1. Do tell it . . . It was so charming . . . And you tell it so well.

M 1. No, I beg of you . . .

W 1. Be nice . . . Tell us some more. It was so sweet. all those little houses . . . I can see them now . . . with the fret-work trimming over the windows . . . like bits of coloured lace . . . And the fences round the gardens where, in the evening, jasmin and acacia . . .

M 1. No, it was idiotic . . . I don't know what got into me . . .

W 2. Not at all, it was enchanting . . . How did you put it? All those childhoods recaptured in the . . . in such . . . in that mellowness . . . It was marvellous, the way you put it . . . What was it exactly? . . . I must try and remember it . . .

M 1. No really, you embarrass me . . . Let's talk about something else, shall we . . . It was ridiculous . . . I don't know what demon got into me . . . I am ridiculous when I let myself be carried away like that . . . when I indulge my occasional lyrical leanings . . . It's stupid, childish . . . At those moments I don't realize what I'm saying . . .

Various voices.

W 3. On the contrary, it was very moving . . .

W 1. It was so . . .

M 1. Do stop everybody, I beg of you. Stop making fun of me . . .

M 2. Making fun of you? Who's making fun of you, for goodness sake . . . I was moved by it too . . . It made me want to see them . . . I'm going there . . . For a long time now . . .

W 3. I, too . . . It was . . . It has something . . . You succeeded in giving . . . Really, it was . . .

M 1. No, no, that's enough, stop it . . .

W 3. It has such poetry . . .

M 1. *(with contained rage, desperate).* Now we have it. So that's it. There it is. That was bound to come out. Now you can be satisfied. You've succeeded. Everything I wanted to avoid *(groaning)* . . . Under no conditions . . . Really *(furious)*, are you blind? Deaf? Totally insensitive? *(Lamenting.)* And yet I did what I could, I warned you, I tried to restrain you, but there's nothing anyone can do, you go right ahead . . . like dumb animals . . . Now you can be satisfied.

W 3. What on earth is the matter? What did I say? Satisfied with what?

M 1. *(icily)*. Nothing. You didn't say a thing. I didn't say a thing. Go right ahead: you can do whatever you like. Spread yourselves. Shout. In any case, it's too late . . . The harm's done . . . When I think . . . *(groaning again)* that it could perhaps have passed unnoticed . . . All right, I made a *faux-pas* . . . I made a mistake . . . but there was nothing fatal about it . . . All that was needed was to let things ride . . . I could have made up for it, I was going to do it . . . But you—you always put your foot in it. God save us from our friends! Now it's too late. Go right ahead. You can do whatever you like.

W 1. What, then? Do what?

M 1. *(imitating her)*. What? what, indeed! You really don't sense what you've started, what has been set in motion . . . by you . . . Oh, *(weeping)* everything I was dreading . . .

W 1. What is it? What were you dreading?

W 2. You know you really make me anxious . . .

M 1. Oh, indeed, I make you anxious . . . It's I who . . .

W 3. Of course it's you. Who do you think it is?

M 1. *(indignant)*. I. I make people anxious? I'm crazy. Of course. It's always the same thing. Whereas you, when it's quite obvious . . . But you can't make me believe . . . You feel it just as much as I do . . . Only you pretend . . . You think it's smart to act as though . . .

M 2. Now, God damn it, as though what? There's no doubt about it, it's true, we must all be poor half-wits, morons . . .

M 1. Oh, I beg of you, don't try to fool me, don't pretend you're innocent. Any normally constituted person feels it right away . . . you're . . . It's like emanations . . . as though someone . . . *(There's a faint laugh)* You hear that? Did you hear him? He couldn't hold it in? It just burst out.

W 1. *(Very dignified)*. That was Jean-Pierre who laughed. You'll admit that most people would have laughed. It's really a scream. Apparently, he was the one.

W 2. Jean-Pierre . . . Why that's impossible, you're not talking about him?

W 3. Jean-Pierre . . . such a quiet, nice chap . . .

M 1. About whom then? Who else would it be?, I ask you . . . Now you are trying to provoke me . . .

M 2. *(quietly)*. Jean-Pierre. That's a good one. Perfect. So it's about him.

M 1. No. It's about the Emperor of China . . . *(sneering)* . . . The Queen of Sheba. The Shah of Persia . . .

W 1. Well, Jean-Pierre, my boy, I congratulate you. You certainly do a lot of things . . . on the quiet . . . You sneak, you . . .

Do you realize what you've started, sitting there, with that innocent look on your face?

W 2.   So it's you, my poor Jean-Pierre, you're the cause of all this excitement . . .

W 3.   Naughty, naughty! . . . Off with his head. He's a holy horror . . . A terrible man who scares people to death. Jean-Pierre! Who's usually so retiring, so well-behaved. Look what you've done, look in what a state you've got our friends here.

M 2.   Jean-Pierre the Terrible. That's what I'm going to call you. The much dreaded gangster. Look at him. By jove, he's threatening us! He's drawn his pistol! *(Laughter).*

W 1.   How about it, Jean-Pierre? Aren't you flattered? You wouldn't have thought it, would you? . . .

M 1.   Forgive them, they know not what they do, pay no attention, for pity's sake . . . Obviously, I never should have . . . I'm the first to realize it. But you must understand . . .

W 2 *(bursts out laughing).*   Do you hear that, Jean-Pierre, you must understand . . . *(with mock sententiousness)* to understand all is to forgive all. Don't forget that, Jean-Pierre.

Mingled laughter and voices.

Yes, you understand, you must be merciful . . .

We beg of you . . .

Have pity, Jean-Pierre, we implore you . . .

M 1.   *(very seriously).* You ask nothing better than to reassure us, isn't that so? I feel certain of it . . . You would do it, in fact, if it were possible . . . And yet it would need so little, just one word. One little word from you and we'd breathe freely again. Everybody would feel reassured, soothed. Because they're all like me, you know, all of them. Only they don't dare show it. That's not their way . . . They're afraid . . . they never take such liberties, you see . . . They play the game, as they say, they think they're obliged to pretend . . . One single word. Some perfectly commonplace little remark . . . Just anything, I assure you, would do. But that's probably beyond you, isn't it? You're 'walled in by your silence', aren't you? I believe that's how they describe it . . . Even if you wanted to come out of it, you couldn't, could you, something keeps you from doing it . . . it's like a dream . . . I understand you, I know what it is . . .

W 2.   *(indignant).* Now, will you please listen to that! I too am perhaps very shy and inhibited, but one thing I do dare to do, and that is to tell you to leave the poor fellow alone. He certainly has patience. If I were he . . .

W 3. He's very, very shy, that's all.

M 1. *(avidly)*. Yes, yes, shy. He's shy. that's it, you've said it,
Madam. That's it. There's no use looking any further.
Why rack our brains? That's it. It's a matter of shyness.
Let's say it's that. Let's keep on saying it. He's shy. It's
wonderful how that reassures us. What a sedative effect those
precise words, those definitions, have on us! We hunt about,
we argue, we grow all excited, then suddenly everything is
perfectly simple. What was it all about anyway? Oh nothing.
Or rather, yes. Something perfectly harmless and familiar.
Now everybody's happy . . . It was shyness.

M 2. *(in mock protest)*. Not on your life. I for one refuse. We're
not going to settle for that. If we did, it would cease to be
funny. I'm enjoying the game. It's beginning to amuse me.
And I refuse, so there *(mock petulance)* to be content with
such apparent banalities, such lazy simplifications as these . . .
No, no, let's be sincere . . . wasn't there something? Some strange
threat? Some mortal danger? You know I adore horror films and
detective stories. We're not going to stop there. Shyness! My eye! A
fig for those ready-made formulas! We're being taken in. What has
shyness got to do with it? You're trying to lull our suspicions.
But the fact is that my instinct for self-preservation has been
aroused, mine too. Now let's see. Let's grab the mystery by the
throat, or rather, go back to the beginning. It was because of a
remark about windows trimmed with fret-work like coloured
lace, and little gardens filled with jasmin . . . that was how the
whole thing started. You can't fool me, I've a good memory . . .
That was what started all those emanations and outbursts, those
choking fits and shouts for help. And now people want to cover
it all up with shyness . . . the way you throw a blanket over a fire .
But it's too late, it's burning, it's crackling . . . don't you hear it?

M 1. *(groaning)*. For pity's sake! Don't listen to him. He's mad.
He doesn't know what he's saying. Just one word. One word of
forgiveness. I know exactly what you thought. I knew it while
I was speaking, I should have restrained myself, but I couldn't.
Your silence . . . it was like a sort of giddiness . . . I was trapped . .
some demon . . . the way we're tempted to speak sacrilegious words
in church . . . Your silence pushed me with all it's weight . . . I
went too far, I overdid it. . .

W 2. He overdid it, do you hear that? Well, Jean-Pierre, say something
I'm beginning to feel frightened myself. You're beginning to get
on my nerves.

W 3. Oh, leave him alone. That'll do. This game has gone on long enough
Let's try something else, shall we? It's no longer funny. What's the
way to get there, you haven't yet told us how you get to that drear
country of yours.

M 1   *(frightened)* I don't know . . . Oh, I don't know anything . . .
Quick, something else . . . Oh, now it's beginning to pile up
it's swelling, Oh, if only I could hide! . . . Such self-assurance
. . . such indelicacy . . . As you see, I'm being punished. And
quite enough. Because of that. That was my mistake, I was
too self-assured. That's what disgusts you, isn't it? It's something
you'll never forgive. I made a botch of things, that's it . . . You
won't stand for that. You yourself are so pure. Angelically pure.
You see what platitudes you make me say. I'm ridiculous.
I don't know what I'm saying any more. As soon as I'm with you
I become emphatic . . . But I understand very well, you know.
You were embarrassed for me. The fact is, it's true, those
windows trimmed with painted lace do mean something to me . . .
and there I went and handed them over . . . and how . . .
in what form! What shoddiness . . . What cheap 'literature' . . .
eh? Isn't that so? That's what it was, wasn't it. It was that?

*During this speech the others have been talking: an occasional
word may be heard above a certain background hum.*

He's extremely nervous . . .

His father before him . . .

In my opinion, to have sent him away . . . to school . . .

My grandmother . . .

Then the words grow more distinct . . .

Cheap literature . . .

Now he's excusing himself to Jean-Pierre . . .

Jean-Pierre the connoisseur . . .

You know the story . . . Why not give him a book . . .

Oh, no, he's got a book . . .

Ha! ha! ha!

Hearty laughter.

M 1.   *(continues).* How stupid they are! They understand
nothing. You don't have to be a great reader to be sensitive and
understanding . . . It's a gift, a talent. Either you have it or you
haven't . . . They're the kind that could read entire libraries . . .
But you, I've always sensed it . . . Words for you . . . You've
never said anything that was commonplace. Never anything vague
or pretentious. Of course, you must use words from time to time.
You have to. To live. A minimum. A word, you know that

95

better than they do, is a serious thing.

M 2. Excuse me for butting in on this private conversation, for breaking up this friendly atmosphere, interrupting this confidential chat *(laughter)* but it seems to me that if there is one thing you shouldn't say to Jean-Pierre, it's just that: that a word is a serious thing. This time, poor devil, he'll never speak again . . . if anyone knows that silence is golden, he's the one . . . he's only too convinced it's true . . .

M 1. You see what they're leading up to . . . You see . . . understand me, I don't think so, but today they tend to say these things very quickly . . . already when they were talking about your shyness . . . It's enough for them to start rummaging about in there, the way people do nowadays. Oh, they never go very deep, you know that. However, they'll surely find . . . To begin with, pride. And from that to saying that you're a man of complexes . . . I must confess that I too . . . sometimes . . . when you grow stubborn . . . but you know, really, I don't believe . . . You with complexes! What nonsense . . . You who . . .

W 4 *(a young voice, very softly)*. You're wrong, you know you'll never get the best of him like that. I went through that myself once . . . And I can tell you there's just one thing to do: pay no attention.

M 1. Pay no attention? You're a fine one . . .

W 4. Yes, I know, *(more softly)* that's what he's counting on . . . that you won't be able to do it. He knows it perfectly . . . that's his hold over you and it amuses him. Whereas you . . . Here's what you must do, listen: By the way, I ran into Bonval. He asked me if I ever saw you, and told me to give you his best . . . I thought he had changed very much, he was grown much older-looking. His wife, on the other hand, is as lovely as ever . . . *(very softly)* go on, try it . . .

M 1 *(in a trembling voice)*. Yes, she's very lovely . . . But if you had known her . . . No, *(tearfully)* I can't . . . You're asking too much of me, it's impossible. You want me to run and I can't even drag myself along, it weighs tons and tons . . . I feel crushed, I'm stifling . . . *(Shouting)* Why don't you speak, say something! If you think it amuses us. People make an effort, do you hear, they don't wear their hearts on their sleeves, they commit themselves, they do, out of charity, out of friendliness, to make contacts, yes indeed, you may look down on me, destroy me, slaughter me, I'll shout it with my last breath: contacts . . . people sacrifice themselves . . . they don't mind saying stupid things . . . They don't give a damn what others think.

W 3.   Do listen, now he's making a scene. He's insulting him,
for goodness sake, it's too funny . . .

W 1.   I'm beginning to think that Jean-Pierre is a strong character,
personally, I should never be able to hold out.

M 2.   I'm taking bets. Will he, or won't he, reply?

M 1 *(in a toneless voice).*   There's no use in betting. He won't.
The gentleman looks down upon us. Our gossip. Our chatter.
Our bad literature. Our shoddy poetry. He, never! He doesn't
want to keep our low company. But I'm going to give your
lordship a piece of my mind. What I really think. They're
right. You are shy. Why look any further? Why all these com-
plications? Our opinion frightens you? Suppose you were to say
something stupid? That could happen, you know. Something
terribly stupid, like everybody else. *(In an affected voice.)* How
awful! . . . What will people say? Imagine, if I were to be taken
for a poor fool, or a moron. That would be unbearable. . .
Whereas, as things are, I occupy the place of honour, I'm the
centre of attention.

W 3.   You know, personally, silent people don't impress me. I
just tell myself that perhaps they have nothing to say.

W 4.   No, I must confess, for me, silent people . . . When I was
fifteen years old I was in love with a man . . . from afar, naturally.
I was only fifteen, he was a friend of my father's, he smoked a
pipe in silence . . . I thought he was . . . just . . . marvellous!

W 3.   Yes, at that age . . . but since then, I can assure you, I've
outgrown it . . .

M 1.   You see, they think you're stupid. That's a fine insult. But
in all probability you don't care a damn. Naturally, it's all the
same to you. Otherwise you'd make an effort. *(Growing softer.)*
You don't give a damn, I was unjust, excuse me, but I know I
sense, have always sensed that you . . . for that reason, with you
. . . When someone else remains silent, I pay no attention. But
you . . . no need to be particularly bright . . . On the contrary,
it weighs upon everything. That's why, frequently, intellectuals
. . . There, I've gone and done it . . . How did I keep from doing
it earlier? . . . But you know you mustn't believe it, not of me . . .
Not I, no, never. I'm not one. I have a horror of them. . . My
scale of values is not what you think. Not at all. More than often,
I feel most uncomfortable when I am with them. They're
insensitive, wooden . . . Oh, Marthe, never fall in love with an
intellectual.

W 4.   Have no fear . . . Go ahead. Keep it up. That's not bad. It
might do . . . That way you may succeed.

M 1.   In fact, I myself, all my friends . . . Always very ordinary

97

people, people who work with their hands . . . They're the ones
who . . . I remember a carpenter . . . I remember . . . However,
I don't know why I say that . . . There are decent people everywhere . . . Among intellectuals, there are . . . But what do we
mean by an intellectual, anyway? Isn't it so? We have to
understand each other . . . You are one, of course . . . for
that matter.

W 1.   I should say so. If Polytechnic isn't a hotbed . . . as they
say . . .

W 2.   If not there, then where are intellectuals to be found?

M 1.   You're right. Where are they to be found? And then, in
reality, what does it mean? No, I said that because there
are people with prejudices . . . as soon as they scent an
intellectual . . . it's as though . . . it's a sort of hatred . . .
they pursue them from childhood on. I once knew a family
. . . Both parents had a sort of repulsion. Poor things, they
have probably produced many a child martyr . . . take
Annie, the Méré's daughter . . . She's the hard working book-
worm kind . . . a real blue-stocking . . . a regular little old
woman . . . I must say she arouses instincts in me . . .

W 2.   Yes, I can understand that . . .

W 3.   I take it then, that there's no hope, you don't want
to tell me how to get there . . . to that place . . . By car
would be the best way . . . only the roads . . .

M 1.   But what is it that's got such a hold on you? What is
there about those wooden houses . . . Do you know what's
the matter with you? I'm like you, in fact, we follow the
style. Just at present, wood, I don't know why . . . puts
me in a state of trance . . . things made of wood . . .
salt-cellars, pepper-pots . . . bare beams on the ceiling. The
other day I read an article that was a scream, about this craze
for old beams . . . I recognized myself . . .

M 2.   That's true, It's probably a reaction against steel and
concrete.

M 1.   However, you have to live with the times. I say that
to myself every time I see a tractor take the place of a
nice farm-wagon . . . you know one of those marvellous
old wagons . . . painted an indescribable blue . . . Oh excuse
me . . . Did you hear that?

Various voices.

No . . .

No, nothing . . .

Hear what?

98

M 1.   A whistle . . . He whistled . . . I heard it . . .

W 3.   Who, he? Jean-Pierre? So it's got you again?

M 1.   I heard it. Do leave us alone. I must speak to him. You used
the word estheticism? . . . You didn't? You didn't say anything?
And yet I could have sworn . . . it's true, I did backslide. A
minute ago, with those farm-wagons . . . That was ridiculous . . .
You know, I've never been able to get rid of my sentimentality.
My little blue flower side . . . *(Laughs sharply)* No matter how I
try to restrain myself, it comes out. Do you know that all my
life . . . I must have missed real happiness because of that.

W 1.   Oh, do tell us . . . How did you miss it? What happiness? Go
ahead, tell us everything.

M 1 *(meekly).*   Everything. I won't hold back anything.
Well, I was very much in love. Really very much. With an adorable
girl, marvellous. She would have been just the one for me. As strong as I am
weak. Her face . . . in fact, Jean-Pierre, when I see him sitting
there, with that firm, hard, pure profile of his, makes me think
of her. She would not have allowed herself the way I do . . . And
do you know, for something as silly as that . . . One day we were
airing ourselves in the little Vert-Galant square on the banks of the
Seine. We were both working on our exams and were questioning
each other on the subject of simple and compound interest in
preparation for the fiscal law exam. And I said: *(he bursts out
laughing)* look at that willow tree, in the light . . . some such silly
thing as that . . . the reflections in the water over there . . . She
didn't so much as turn her head, but continued to pore over
her notes . . . I said it again . . . But she only questioned me
sternly on the subject of compound interest . . . Well, I felt
that everything was cracking up . . . I never could explain it.
It was all over. She never understood. My entire family.
Hers. They were so pleased . . . 'It's pathological', I remember,
my father said that, he was furious. With me it's pathological.
It's true, he was right . . . That's why . . .

M 2.   Oh, that is funny. You are a scream. They really do mean
a lot to you, don't they, those little lace-trimmed windows of
yours . . .

M 1.   But you see yourself where it got me. Since then I've often
regretted . . . I have probably wasted my life . . . Did you hear
that? It sounded as though he made a noise. It seemed to me
that he laughed, didn't he?

M 2.   Of course he laughed. You really are funny.

M 1.   He laughed, that's certain. I made him laugh. Why, I'm really
delighted. What would I not give him? He has only to take, it's all his.
All. His. If only he'll laugh. Now there, I've cheered you up, haven't I?
I make you laugh . . . That may perhaps remind you of something,

you too. Something funny . . . in your life . . . It would be
such a pleasure, it would be such an honour . . . you don't
have to contribute so much. Whereas I *(suddenly with great
dignity)* What I have given is a lot . . . without seeming so
(a stifled sign) . . . it's a large piece . . . But you, just a little
one . . . A tiny bit . . . A crumb . . . And we shall be satisfied
. . . But it's down dog, isn't it? You're against such
promiscuity. You didn't ask for anything, did you? Why did
I have to come and force it on you? You're drawing aside.
Not so close. Oh he's moving even farther away, stop it.
(Turning to the others.) Why don't you do something, for
goodness sake, why don't you react after all, it's becoming
unbearable, it's indecent . . .

W 1.   That's true, Jean-Pierre, say something . . .

W 2.   Quite obviously Jean-Pierre looks down upon us . . .

W 3.   Jean-Pierre you are a source of distress . . .

Laughter

M 2.   Now there, Jean-Pierre, be quiet . . .

Renewed laughter.

M 1.   They're teasing you . . . But I'm going to tell you something:
In a way I understand you. These are things concerning which
one should tread lightly. For you those little fret-work trimmings
are sacred. They're taboo. They should be handled the way one
does the things on an altar table, dressed in priestly robes. This
profanation makes you indignant. You want to show me that
you disapprove. You remain aloof. That's it. Silence does
not give consent. You don't like to see things defiled . . . How I
admire you. I like people to be uncompromising, stern. You are
a poet. A real one . . . A poet . . . that's what you are . . .

W 3.   There we have it. Always these extremes. A while ago you
were a clod. Now it's Baudelaire. You know, Jean-Pierre, what
you're doing there is quite a feat.

W 1.   Personally, if I had the strength of character to restrain
myself, I'd say nothing, ever.

W 2.   You know George Sand . . . That was her charm. It seems
she never opened her mouth.

W 1.   Yes, she used to smoke big cigars. I can just see her: with
her eyes half closed, and that mysterious expression on her
face. It's not surprising that all her contemporaries were
under her spell.

M 2.   You forget one little detail: she also had her work. That
filled her silence.

M 1.   No, no, you don't understand. That was her weakness.

Without having accomplished anything, that's a much greater feat. Do nothing — that's quite something. To just sit silent, and never have done a thing. Excuse me, I'm not speaking of you, I know you work, I admire your work, as you know . . . All these. . . For me that's a closed book. No, I'm generalizing. But it's really something when people have done nothing at all, absolutely nothing, and they reach the top merely by means of the pressure they exert . . .

W 3. You know, it's strange, it's contagious, you've given me your disease . . . I too, now, am beginning to feel . . . it's like some sort of gas . . . No, Jean-Pierre, stop it . . .

W 2. Jean-Pierre, hoo-ooh, look at the birdie . . . Now smile . . . once more . . . hoo-ooh, smile . . . There we are . . .

W 3. He really did smile . . . I saw him . . .

M 2. That's true, I saw him too. He smiled. It was very clear. We amuse him, that's obvious. He thinks we're funny. We *are* funny. Fascinated. Imprisoned. He has trapped us. This silence is like a net. He's watching us wriggle . . .

W 1. I'm going to do the same. Let's all do it. Let's play that game. Silence. Everybody be silent, very dignified . . .

W 2. But . . .

W 3. Shhh . . .

Silence.

W 2 *(bursts out laughing).* No, count me out. I can't keep it up! I can't bear it, my tongue is itching . . .

M 2. The fact is that we're not up to it. No good. That's certain. It's not worth a farthing, our silence isn't. Has no effect, on me, in any case.

The others.

On me either.

Nor on me.

Not at all heavy.

Lighter than air . . . Rare.

M 1 *(avidly).* You see, what did I tell you? With him it's heavy, full to bursting. It's incredible what there is in it. I'm submerged by it. It gets me down.

M 2. To tell the truth, I think you contribute considerably to it. You fill it with all kinds of things which probably . . .

W 1. It's well known that we only lend to the rich. As for me, I could remain silent till the end of time . . .

M 1. Now I know what you reproach me with. You're right. It's a

101

matter of form. As I said before . . . But I have just understood
. . . it's the form. To get you to accept my little fret-work trimmings,
I should have presented them to you politely, the way they should
be, on a silver platter, with white gloves on. In a book,
with an expensive-looking cover. Handsomely printed. In a well
polished style. I'm lazy, as you said, I can hear you, a good-for-
nothing, I'm a gate-crasher, without making an effort, I wanted
to move you, astound you, treat myself to a little success,
just like that, merely by talking. I should have had to work at it,
by the sweat of my brow, spend sleepless nights. Find a style for
my fret-work. Eh? isn't that so? That's what you can't forgive.
Everything in it's place. In a collection of poems, you would
have deigned? . . . No excuse me . . . Why deigned . . .
You might perhaps, really have enjoyed, in solitude, this
quintessence, this nectar . . .

W 1.   There now. This silence was golden. It will force you to write
us a nice poem. You're going to write us a lovely poem on
those fret-work trimmings. On those . . .

W 2.   Impossible. You can't. Overdone. Deadly commonplace. The sub-
exhausted. It was all right . . .

M 1.   So there. Do you hear? It's no good. Trash. All right in a convers-
Just barely. Our conversations. A man of refined tastes is nauseated
as you see. I might say that you have a salutary influence. People like
you are necessary. They keep things moving . . . They carry high
the flame . . . *(suddenly, he starts to shout).* Lies, lies, monstrous lies
I'm crazy, that's so much delirious generosity. You are of no use at a
It's not that. What am I thinking of? What have you ever done that
gives you the right . . . I don't have to learn from you. You hate
poetry. You hate all that kind of thing in every form or shape,
whether in the raw, or elaborately transformed. You are practical.
And what you call sentimentality . . . Oh, there's not room for the tw
of us in this world. I can't live where you are. I stifle, I perish . . .
You are too destructive. I'm going to make you beg for mercy. I'm
going to force you to your knees. I'm going to describe those lace
trimmed windows, and you'll be obliged, whether you want to or
not, you'll be forced . . . He repeated forced? You said 'forced',
and laughed.

W 1.   No, it was I who said it. Like an echo.

M 1.   It was not, he too said it. I heard him. He said it, 'forced?' and
laughed. 'Forced, I,' — that's what he said. 'Forced?' Who can force
him? You can read him whatever you like . . . nobody can force him
feel admiration.

W 2.   Oh, let's not exaggerate. Jean-Pierre has plenty of taste.
He knows his classics by heart.

M 1 *(wailing).* But, how shall I . . . How do you expect . . . How could
compete? I'm not well-known, and he only bows to . . . only

recognizes . . . The gentleman is a snob. He must have fame. Practical people are like that. How much do you make out of it? Eh? At the end of the year? What had you made out of those little lace-trimmed windows of yours?

Silence.

W 3 *(in a slightly unreal voice)* There are those . . . whose mere presence paralyses people's voices and hearts . . . Both their voices and their hearts . . .

W 2. Oh, how charming! Who said that?

W 3. Balzac. Balzac said that. It just came to me . . It has struck me. He wrote — I think it's in Louis Lambert: 'Those who attain to a higher plane without deserving it, paralyse by their presence people's voices and hearts.'

M 1 *(astounded)*. He said that? Balzac? Good Lord: And you didn't mention it? You didn't say it earlier! And I'm supposed to be crazy! I! When a century ago, Balzac . . . I didn't make him say it, did I? He saw clearly, he felt as I do . . . he understood. A single piece of evidence is enough to prove . . . and who had furnished it? Balzac! Neither more nor less! If Balzac were here . . . *(Delighted laughter.)* Of course . . . It's simply that . . . in fact, I sensed it, I suspected it, this person has wormed his way into our midst without the right to do so, he's not one of us, he's an impostor. He stops . . .

M 2. I don't know whether he stops people's heart or not, but as regards their voices, it seems to me that yours . . . Never did you talk so much . . .

M 1. Why, what's the matter? Why, why he's standing, oh I beg of you, don't go. Not at this point, not like that . . . Help . . . oh, I've lost my foothold, I'm drifting, alone between earth and sky . . . oh . . .

W 1. He's had enough. *(Laughter.)* His feelings are ruffled. No wonder.

M 1. Ruffled! Oh no, your feelings aren't ruffled. Say they're not, say . . . I'd do anything. He yawned, he's stretching himself, we bore him. What did I tell you, we're the unworthy ones. We are on the lower plane. It's us. He's bored with us . . .

W 2. Well, what does that prove? As it happens the people on the lower plane are bored with . . .

M 1. Oh, please, no more subtle remarks, this is not the moment . . . Lower, higher, what do we mean by such distinctions? We're alike, brothers, all equal . . . and then suddenly in our midst . . . one of us . . . oh, I can't stand it . . . look at him cracking his knuckles . . . the face he's making . . . in a second he's going to . . . his eyes are wandering . . . he's getting up . . . He's already elsewhere . . . oh . . . oh . . . Come . . . come, all of you, I beg of you let's try. Jean-Pierre, I'm going to tell you . . . No, have no fear not about fret-work trimming, this has nothing to do with those

blooming windows . . . They can go to hell . . . *(Laughter.)*
I'm going to tell you something really funny. A story. I know
lots of them. I love to tell them, as well as listen to them. You
know, the one about the two friends . . . do you know about
it? They always told each other the same stories. Finally, they
decided to number them. All they had to do was to say a
number: 27, for instance . . . and the other, after a moments thought,
would burst out laughing. He would answer: 18, and then the first
friend would laugh heartily . . . that's funny, isn't it?

W 2.⎫
W 3. ⎬ Ha! ha! ha!
M 2.⎭

W 2. That's funny, don't you think so Jean-Pierre?

M 2 *(slightly ill at ease).*   You know he's like the young man at the
party — this is another good one — everybody was laughing.
The hostess looked at him: 'Why aren't you laughing?' And
he replied: Thank you very much but I've already laughed. . . '

M 1.   Ha! ha! ha! That is good, that's perfect, I didn't know
that one . . . But I'm going to tell you another that somebody just told me . . . A little boy just came home from
Sunday school . . . and his father asked him: 'What did the
preacher talk about today? 'He talked about sin,' the little
boy said. 'Sin? What did he say about it?' The boy thought
for a moment, then said: 'He was agin it . . . '

General laughter.

W 1.   Ha! ha! I'm like that . . . My husband says I always
talk like that. It's all right . . . When I've been to an exhibition
or read a book. Even when I was a child I was like that little
boy. My father asked me what I was studying in history and
I said . . . *(she begins to hesitate)* . . . in fact I don't why I
tell this story, it's somewhat similar . . . the point is the
same . . . however . . . I said, 'We're studying the Renaissance'
. . . And since I seemed a bit vague . . . my father hated that
. . . he said: 'And what is the Renaissance, you don't seem to
know what it was.' . . . And I answered: 'Oh, it was all
right . . . ' *(People laugh)* But that's stupid. I don't know why
. . .

M 1 *(furious).* You don't know? Well, then, I'll tell you. Because
of this gentleman. You've caught it. You're infected. It's
got you. He's drawing you to him . . .

Voices.

He's drawing her to him.

104

M 1. And what about me? Do I have to tell those stories of mine?
I know them well . . . I have no desire to shine, I assure you . . .
There's no question of it. *(Bitter)* We haven't come to that.
It's to entertain his lordship. May he deign to forgive me. But
what wouldn't one do? No effort is too great: however
ridiculous, however humiliating . . . Anything . . . She, poor
dear, lost her balance. You feel you'd accept damnation itself.
You'd sell your very soul . . . as I did . . . Let him take it . . .
W 3 *(begging, whispering).* Yes . . . Yes, take it, I can't hold it
back, you are sucking it up . . . it's rising, here it is . . . I make
you a present of it . . . I lay it in offering at your feet . . . Do
you like it?
W 2. And mine? Like this? Sad? No, you don't like it.
W 3. Not sad? Disillusioned? Nostalgic? No, not like that?
W 4. On the contrary, funny. Amusing. Very gay. And bold . . .
You'll see. I'm going to . . .
M 2. No, comical, a bit ludicrous. I know . . . he'll like that.
Wait a moment, I'm going to tell you . . . you don't mind,
Marthe, if I tell it?
W 4 *(sad and hopeless).* Of course . . . anything you want . . . How
can I refuse? If you think . . . only I'd be surprised . . .
M 2. I too, to tell the truth. But we have to try . . . Believe me,
we've nothing to lose by it . . .
W 4. Very well, go ahead.
M 2. Well, you know Marthe can do some funny things. As you
know, Marthe's a good swimmer, but she has one fault, she
never knows how to touch the bottom . . .
M 1. He looks surprised, he's watching you. Why, out of a clear
sky? You could have prepared us . . . Like the man who wanted
to tell his horse story . . . He tried to lead the conversation to
. . . but it couldn't be done . . . So finally . . .
M 2. No, no preparation is needed . . . Why? Why waste time? It
exasperates him, he's getting impatient . . . Very well, then. Last
summer, at the beach, Marthe was swimming at low tide . . . She
called out . . . started to shout . . . Help! Everybody jumped up
. . . people began to collect . . .
W 4. Oh, began to collect . . . We were alone . . .
M 2 *(severely).* No, Marthe. You know perfectly that there were
lots of people. I called out to her . . . Stand up straight! Stand
up, I tell you . . . I kept shouting . . . Everybody began to roar
with laughter: She's not out of her depth . . . Anyway, it was a
scream . . .
M 1 *(Sad).* No, you see it's no use. There's no use in sacrificing
yourself. It's sickening . . .

W 4. I think it's getting more and more so.
W 1. That's true. In fact I feel like leaving. I'd like to go.
It's getting me down . . .
W 2. A feeling . . . I, too . . .
W 3. Like a sort of loneliness . . .
W 4. I'd feel safer, less lost, even on a desert island. . .
W 2. I too. You feel dejected. I've lost heart.
W 3. Voices and hearts . . . How true that is . . . It's a law . . .
You can't go against it . . . Voices and hearts . . . His presence
paralyses . . .
W 1. I feel as though I'd been emptied . . . everything in me has
been sucked off . . .
W 2. A small blot absorbed by a blotter . . .

Long silence, sighs . . .

M 1 *(firmly).*   Well, my friends. Well, it's like this *(Determinedly).*
as I was saying, there are houses there like the ones in fairy-
tales. With window trimmings like painted lace. And gardens
full of acacias . . . Yes, everything there is untouched. Everything
is replete with childhood . . . A certain ingenuousness overspreads
everything. And in the little churches and chapels . . . really
for them alone, believe me, it's worth the trip . . . Even the
most forlorn among them contain real treasures . . . frescoes . . .
amazing . . . *(louder)* of Byzantine origin . . . *(Articulating more
and more distinctly.)* Like the ones in certain parts of Macedonia,
(somewhat mechanically) near Gracanica and Decani . . .
Nowhere else, not even in Mistra, can you see such perfect examples.
There's one village in particular, I forget the name, but I can
find it on the map . . . where there are some exceptionally lovely
ones . . . incomparably rich . . .This is a liberated form of
Byzantine art, it fairly explodes . . . *(with self-assurance)* in fact
there exists a remarkably well-documented book on the subject
with superb illustrations . . . by Labovic . . .
JEAN-PIERRE.   By Labovic?
M 2.⎤
W 1.⎥ Did you hear him?
W 2.⎬Oh, did you hear him?
W 3.⎥ He spoke!
W 4.⎦
M 2. You see, about certain precise things. Serious ones. Byzantine
art . . . because that, after all, is something very different from . . .
(Mockingly.)
M 1 *(impassive).*   Yes, it's an excellent book. Very well done.
I can recommend it to you. Because in order to really profit
by a trip like that, it's better to prepare it.

106

JEAN-PIERRE.   Labovic, you said? Who's the publisher?

M 1.   Cordier, I believe . . . I can let you have the reference.

ALL *(delighted, enchanted)*. { Oh, he's talking
He's asking questions . . .
That interests him . . .

M 1.   Why shouldn't Byzantine art interest him?

W 1.   Oh, because a little while ago . . .

M 1.   What about a little while ago?

W 2.   Why you yourself . . .

M 1.   I myself what?

W 3.   His silence . . .

M 1.   What silence?

W 4 *(ill at ease)*. It was a bit . . . It seemed to me . . . *(Hesitates a second, then)* Oh, nothing . . . I don't know . . .

M 1.   Then neither do I. I didn't notice anything.

Contemporary Playwrights:

TREVOR GRIFFITHS (England)
Occupations (also *The Big House*)
Apricots (in Gambit 29)

PAUL FOSTER (U.S.A.)
Tom Paine
Balls (also *The Recluse, Hurrah for the Bridge,*
The Hessian Corporal)
Heimskringla ! or *The Stoned Angels*
Marcus Brutus (also *Silver Queen Saloon*)

EUGENE IONESCO (France)
Plays Vol. 1 (*The Chairs The Bald Prima Donna, The*
Lesson, Jacques)
Plays Vol. 2 (*Amedee, The New Tenant, Victims of Duty*)
Plays Vol. 3 (*The Killer, Improvisation, Maid to Marry*)
Plays Vol. 4 (*Rhinoceros, The Leader, The Future is in*
Eggs)
Plays Vol. 5 (*Exit the King, The Motor Show, Foursome*)
Plays Vol. 6 (*A Stroll in the Air, Frenzy for Two*)
Plays Vol. 7 (*Hunger and Thirst, Anger, Salutations,*
The Picture)
Plays Vol. 8 (*Here comes the Chopper, The Oversight,*
The Foot of the Wall)
Plays Vol. 9 (*Macbett, The Mime, Learning to Walk*)
Plays Vol. 10 (*Oh What a Bloody Circus, The Hard*
Boiled Egg)
Plays Vol. 11 (*The Man with the Luggage, The Duel*)

MUSTAPHA MATURA (West Indies)
As Time Goes By (*also Black Pieces*)
Play Mas

RENE DE OBALDIA (France)
Wind in the Branches of the Sassafras
Plays Vol. 1 (*Jenusia, and Seven Impromptus For Leisure*)
Plays Vol. 2 (*Satyr of La Villette, Wide Open Spaces, The*
Unknown General)
Plays Vol. 3 (*Two Women for One Ghost, The Babysitter,*
The Jellyfish's Banquet)   forthcoming
Plays Vol. 4 (*Mr. Klebs and Rosalie, And Suddenly there*
came the Bang !)   forthcoming

PABLO PICASSO (France)
Desire Caught by the Tail
The Four Little Girls

BARRY RECKORD (England)
Skyvers (also *X*)   forthcoming

NATHALIE SARRAUTE (France)
Collected Plays Vol. 1 (*It is There, It's Beautiful, Izzum,*
The Lie and *Silence*)

ROLAND TOPOR (France)
Leonardo Was Right

ROGER VITRAC (France)
Victor (also *The Trafalgar Coup* and *Médor*)   forthcoming

PETER WEISS (Germany)
The Marat-Sade
The Investigation
Discourse on Vietnam

HEATHCOTE WILLIAMS (England)
The Immortalist
AC/DC
The Speakers (in Gambit 25)
The Truth Dentist   forthcoming

SNOO WILSON (England)
Pignight (with *Blowjob*)
Reason (in Gambit 29)

Complete list of published plays will be sent on request

JOHN CALDER (PUBLISHERS) LTD.
18 Brewer Street, London W1R 4AS

A Calderbook CB 354 £4.95

COLLECTED PLAYS

Nathalie Sarraute

Translated by Maria Jolas and Barbara Wright

It Is There * **It's Beautiful** * **Izzum** * **The Lie** * **Silence**

Nathalie Sarraute is best known as a novelist whose investigations of human behaviour and the motivations behind it have created a new kind of social novel. The doyenne of the *nouveau roman* group of post-war French writers, she had already established herself in the thirties as an experimental writer with a new approach to the observation of human nature. Her first book *Tropisms*, a series of short sketches demonstrating how behavioural tics often give away what is really happening behind the facades we assume, became the model for all her subsequent work including her eight important novels.

These five plays translate her special technique onto the stage. They are plays that dramatize inter-personal and inter-social relationships, refining subtlety and nuance to an incredible degree and depicting the ways in which human beings influence each other and the antagonisms and irritations that we all experience, often without knowing why. The confrontation of generations, of different class, aesthetic or educational backgrounds, the ways in which we come to understand each other, despise each other, deceive each other — whether tolerated or not — is the raw material of these plays, all of which have been successfully staged in France by the Renaud-Barrault Company and in many other countries in translation. *Silence* and *The Lie* have been seen in London.

The five plays are printed in anti-chronological order, with the most recent first. This was translated by Barbara Wright, one of Britain's most distinguished translators of important contemporary French literature, and the others by Maria Jolas, for many years a close friend and translator of Nathalie Sarraute, who is also remembered as the only surviving close friend and patron of James Joyce.

Cover design by Brian Paine with a photograph of the author by Jerry Bauer.

JOHN CALDER (PUBLISHERS) LTD.
18 Brewer Street, London W1R 4AS

O9-BGN-296

ISBN 0 7145 3713 6